THE LAMENT OF EVE

by

JOHANNA MANLEY

MONASTERY BOOKS

Menlo Park, California 1993

Library of Congress Cataloging-in-Publication Data

Manley, Johanna, 1927-
    The lament of Eve / by Johanna Manley
        p.   cm.
    Includes bibliographical references and index.
    ISBN 0-9622536-2-6
    1. Bible. O.T. Genesis I-V--Criticism, interpretation, etc.
    2. Eve (Biblical figure) 3. Orthodox Eastern Church--Liturgy.
    4. Orthodox Eastern Church--Doctrines. I. Eve. (Biblical figure)
    II. Title.
    BS1235.2.M36   1993
    222'. 1106--dc20   92-45056
                                                                CIP

THE LAMENT OF EVE

© Copyright 1993 Johanna Manley

ISBN 0-9622536-2-6

Published by MONASTERY BOOKS

287 Bay Road, P.O. Box 2579, Menlo Park, CA 94025-2579.

TABLE OF CONTENTS

Introduction   ii

PROLOGUE - THE STORY OF EVE   1
   Selections from Genesis 1 to 5 and Church Fathers'
   Commentary

THE LAMENT OF EVE   51

EPILOGUE: PART I: 73
   Letter to a Spiritual Daughter:
   LESSONS IN DIVINE AND CHRISTIAN LOVE

            PART II   100
   THE SONG OF EVE AND HER DESCENDANTS

            PART III   107
   Psalm 118: THE WAY, THE TRUTH AND
          THE LIFE

Index of Church Fathers   151

Bibliography   152

INTRODUCTION

The *Lament of Eve* attempts an exegesis of sections of the first five chapters of Genesis based on combining commentary of the Fathers of the Church. Saint Silouan of Mount Athos gave us *Adam's Lament*, as brought to us by Archimandrite Sophrony of St. John the Baptist Community in Essex, England. But since in recent times women have hoped for more expression of their roles and being, the emphasis here is on Eve. In her *Lament*, Eve is addressing her progeny in her old age, up to and including Lamech.[1]

This book is especially addressed to Orthodox Christians for reading during Great Lent. The readings in the lectionary during the period before Holy Week are from Genesis, Isaiah and Proverbs. Also, the theme of *The Lament of Eve* is full of compunction.

To minimize the risk of theological error, certain groundrules were first laid down. One of these is to provide a Prologue citing all pertinent passages of the Scripture and associated patristic commentary for the reader's preliminary review. Moreover, to tie any significant statements in the *Lament* firmly to their source, a code system was devised. The numbers in [ ] in the ensuing *Lament* will be seen to correspond to numbered sections or paragraphs in the Prologue, serving to point to their source.

An Epilogue was added. Since the *Lament* leaves Eve yearning and hoping for restoration, and the Orthodox Holy Saturday depiction on the front cover of this book shows Christ raising Adam and Eve from their tombs, it appeared that a bridge in time was needed to show, through our hindsight many millenia later, the fulfilment of this desire and hope through Christ. Indeed, since many of us - like Adam and Eve - yearn to know how to make our own restoration possible by the grace of God, the Epilogue includes instructions towards this end for us all.

Epilogue Part I is from *The Collected Works of Bishop Nikolai Velimirovich* of thrice-blessed memory. It is an excerpt from the book *Kassiana*, a letter written by Archimandrite Callistratus, an Abbot of Mileševo Monastery in Bosnia-Herzogovina to his spiritual daughter, the nun Kassiana, presumably in the 19th century. Before becoming a nun and taking the name Kassiana, she had been named "hunchbacked Julie." In her despair at her physical unsightliness and all its attendant consequences, this woman had dramatically blasphemed God before the abbot, and, after chastising her, he calms her, teaches her, and finally tonsures her a nun. She then becomes immersed in service to God through love of children. The letter comprises one hundred and two "*Lessons in Divine and Christian*

Love", and it is a document on love rivalling the profundity of St. Maximus the Confessor's *Four Centuries on Love*, and approaching even St. Paul's memorable message to the Corinthians (1 Cor. 13).

Epilogue Part II brings us back to Eve with *The Song of Eve and her Descendants*. This is based on the nine Scriptural Odes which the Orthodox Church commemorates in its Matins and other services. Eight of these are from the Old Testament as indicated, and one, the ninth, from the Gospel of St. Luke. The Church uses these expressions of thanksgiving and praise and acknowledgment of God's help and salvific guidance to express its profounder truths. Eve, in hindsight, is symbolically celebrating the effect of the *fiat* of the Virgin Mary and salvation through Jesus Christ.

This section is not intended to be developed into a Canon in the church. In the spirit of the conceptual presentation of the main section, *The Lament of Eve*, it merely uses the Church's own mode of expression and format to lead the reader from the hopelessness of Eve's burial in sin to the glorious hope offered to us all in the Resurrection of our Lord and Savior Jesus Christ. It brings us ultimately to the Church's triumphant Paschal *Troparion*, "Christ is risen from the dead, trampling down death by death and upon those in the tombs bestowing life," depicted through liturgical iconography on the front cover. This joyful hope, is after all, the end point of our lenten journey, as epitomized also in the Holy Saturday reading from Ezekiel (37:1-14) about the reviving of the dry bones.

Since this end point is not reached without our own effort, Epilogue Part III is intended to help us on our journey and in our daily struggles towards spiritual growth. It is an extract and condensation from *Grace for Grace: The Psalter and the Holy Fathers* (see Bibliography), here entitled *The Way, the Truth and the Life*. This portion presents Psalm 118 (Septuagint [119 KJV]) together with commentary from the early Church Fathers. The Fathers considered this psalm to be important as an instruction book on how to live a God-pleasing life. The Fathers' interpretations tie it to the salvific effect of the incarnation of Christ.

Since the Church Fathers generally tended to use the Septuagint version of the Scriptures, the Bible passages used herein are from two sources, both derived from the Septuagint. For the Epilogue, Part III, *The Psalter According to the Seventy* was used, translated by the Holy Transfiguration Monastery in Brookline, Massachusetts © 1974. All remaining Old Testament extracts are from *The Septuagint with Apocrypha* published by Hendrickson Publishers, Peabody, MA, translated by Sir Lancelot C. L. Brenton.

It will be noted that in this book, all Scripture has been accepted at face value and within its own context. As such it preserves its own integrity and still serves as a mirror even for us in modern times to see ourselves and meditate on our own salvation and desired *theosis*. [2]

Modern Biblical study, though fascinating, has been ignored, and the many other levels of meaning have been left to scholars far more erudite than the author. St. John Chrysostom and all the other early Fathers show no awareness of differences in style or passages as from a Yahwist or a priestly writer, or others, and for this particular conceptual study they are considered to be irrelevant. The Fathers often speak in terms of typology, and this style of thought does lend itself to the present exercise.

Our major object in confining ourselves to the mode of presentation of the Fathers is to continue to offer the beauty, robust practical and universal application, profundity and freshness of their writings to this age.

My book, *The Bible and the Holy Fathers for Orthodox*, (see Bibliography) regretfully lacked sufficient material to do justice to Old Testament readings. Some of the material is now available in English, the remainder has had to be translated. God willing, commentary on Isaiah and Job will follow.

My deep and sincere gratitude for extensive help is acknowledged to Nun Verna Harrison (Ph.D., Visiting Professor in Patristics at St. Vladimir's Seminary), Mother Susanna (Payne), Rachel Hales, and several proofreaders who wish to be nameless.

My special dedication is to the *Theotokos*, who helped me with her intercession in my dire need, and who has given me the courage in my ignorance and inadequacy to attempt this book.

NOTES

1. The chart on p. 50, based on Genesis 5, shows that Eve would have lived to know Lamech, but not his son, Noah - assuming she lived the same length of time as Adam.

2. Deification or divinization - the final goal at which every Christian must aim. For Orthodoxy, according to Bishop Kallistos Ware in *The Orthodox Church* (p. 236), man's salvation and redemption mean his deification.

3. Collections of books referred to in the Church Fathers' commentary by abbreviation are as follows - see Bibliography for further details.

ACW = Ancient Christian Writers, Paulist Press;
ANF = Ante-Nicene Fathers;
C = *Commentaire sur le Psaume 118*, Vol. I by Hilary of Poitiers, SC;
CUA = Catholic University of America;
LCP = *La Chaîne Palestinienne sur le Psaume 118*, Vol. I, SC;
NPNF = The Nicene and Post-Nicene Fathers;
OTP = *On the Psalms* by Augustine of Hippo, NPNF FS, Vol. VIII;
SC = Sources Chrétiennes.

PROLOGUE - THE STORY OF EVE

GENESIS, CHAPTER 1 - Selected Verses (Septuagint)

[1] *1:26: And God said, Let Us make man according to Our image and likeness, and let them have dominion over the fish of the sea, and over the flying creatures of heaven, and over the cattle and all the earth, and over all the reptiles that creep on the earth.* [1, 2, 3, 4, 5*]

1:27: And God made man, according to the image of God He made him, male and female He made them. [1, 4, 5]

1:28: And God blessed them, saying, Increase and multiply, and fill the earth and subdue it, and have dominion over the fish ... [1, 6, 7, 8, 9, [88]]

1:29: And God said, Behold I have given to you every seed-bearing herb sowing seed which is upon all the earth, and every tree which has in itself the fruit of seed that is sown, to you it shall be for food.

1:30: All the wild beasts of the earth ...which has in itself the breath of life, even every green plant for food; and it was so. [10]

1:31 ...And there was evening and there was morning, the sixth day.

The Fathers on Genesis 1

1. St. Basil the Great:

[2] (Text #3). "Let Us make man according to Our image and likeness." From this, begin to know yourself. These words had not yet been applied to any of the creations. Light appeared, and the commandment was simple. God said, "Let there be light." The firmament came into being and there was no deliberation concerning its coming to be. The luminaries came to be without any previous deliberation regarding them. The sea and the boundless ocean: a command and they were brought into being ...The wild beasts ...one word, and they had come to be. At this point, man does not yet exist, and there is deliberation regarding man. God did not say as He did for the others, "Let there be man!"

Note the dignity befitting you. He has not initiated your origin by a command, but there has been counsel in God to determine how to introduce into life this living being worthy of honor. "Let us make man," the wise One deliberates, the artisan ponders. Do you not fall short of His art, and does not He, with care offer to His masterpiece its [intended] achievement: perfection and exactitude? Or does he not wish to show you as perfect in relation to God?

---

* See plain numbers next to names of church fathers below.

(Text #4). You have learned that there were two persons, the one who spoke and one to whom the words were addressed. Why did God not say "Make," but "Let us make man"?

It is so you will recognize the sovereignty, so that in recognizing the Father, you may not deny the Son; He wants you to know that the Father has created through the Son and that the Son has created through the Father's will, and that you should glorify the Father in the Son, and the Son in the Holy Spirit. Also, you have been made their common work that you may worship both in common, not dividing the worship but uniting the Divinity ...

He did not say, "The gods made man," but "God made." Yet the personal properties of the Father are His own, those of the Son are His own, and those of the Holy Spirit are His own.

(Text #5). So how are we in the image of God?

Let us purify ourselves of a vulgar heart, of uneducated perception and of stupid conceptions of God. If we have been created in the image of God, will anyone say God is in the same form as ours, having eyes, ears, a head, hands ...Do not imagine any form for Him. Do not diminish, in the manner of the Jews, Him who is great; do not confine God within corporeal concepts, do not delimit Him to the measure of your mind. He is inapprehensible in His grandeur. Reflect on something grand, augment it to the maximum you can conceive, and increase it even more: be persuaded that your own thought will never attain to that which is infinite. Do not imagine Him in terms of form - God is understood from His power. Because of the simplicity of His nature, His grandeur cannot be quantified. He is everywhere and transcends all; and intangible, invisible, he escapes our mind's grasp. No greatness can circumscribe Him; no form can enclose Him; no power can measure Him; no time-span can encompass Him; no boundary can limit Him. Nothing pertaining to God is the same as it is for us.

(Text #6). In what sense, then, does the Scripture say that we have been made in the image of God?

As we learn the things of God, let us understand those things that concern us. We do not possess that which is in His image in bodily form for the bodily form is such that the incorruptible does not imprint its pattern on the corruptible, and the corruptible is not the image of the incorruptible. The body grows and abates, ages and changes. It is in one state in youth, different in age, one way in health, another in sickness, one in fear, another in joy; it is one way in abundance, another in want, one in peace, another in war ...

How, then, can that which changes resemble the unchanging? How can what has no stability be like that which eternally remains the same?... Again, in what does the human preeminence consist? In the superiority of reason. All that is lacking in the capability of the body is amply supplied by the structure of the intellect ...

(Text #7). Man is said to be in the image of God, and the mind is the man. Listen to the words of the Apostle: "though our outward man perish, yet the inward man is renewed day by day" (2 Cor. 4:16).

In what manner?

I distinguish two men, one that appears outwardly, and the other invisible under cover of the man who appears: the interior man. We have an interior being, and we are twofold in some ways, but, truthfully speaking, we are the interior being. For I see myself as the interior man: that which is exterior is not myself, but mine. Neither is the hand myself, but I am the reasoning principle of the soul. The hand is a part of man. Likewise, the body is the instrument of the man, the instrument of the soul, but principally the man in himself is the soul.

"Let Us make man according to Our image," that is to say: let Us give him the superiority of reason (δώσωμεν αὐτῷ λόγου περιουσίαν).

(Text #8). For the passions are not included in the image of God, but rather reason, the master of the passions ...

It is in the foremost place that we have discerned the power of the commandment. Man, you are a living being, made to command! Why do you enslave yourself to the passions? Why do you lower your dignity and become a slave to sin? Why do you make of yourself a prisoner of the devil? You have been chosen to be the prince of creation, yet you have rejected the nobility of your real nature.

Sur l'Origine de l'Homme. Sources Chrétiennes No. 160, pp. 171-185. © Les Éditions du Cerf, Paris 1970.

[3] (Text #16). "Let us make man according to Our image and likeness." We possess the one by our creation; we are conformed to the other by free choice (ἐκ προαιρέσεως κατορθοῦμεν). In our original fashioning, it has been given to us to be born in the image of God. By our preference the being in likeness to God forms itself in us. We are capable of possessing that which accords with our choice, but our own actions bring it to actuality. If, in creating us, the Lord had not taken the precaution in advance of saying "Let us make" and "likeness," if He had not bestowed on us the potential to come to be in the likeness, we would not by our own power have acquired likeness to God. Nevertheless, here He has created us potentially able to be like God. In giving us the potential to resemble God, He has permitted us to be the artisans of likeness to God, in order that we should receive the recompense of our labor, so that we should not be like portraits made by a painter, inert objects, but to the end that the result of our resemblance should not redound to the praise of another.

3

(Text #17). "Be ye therefore perfect, even as your Father which is in heaven is perfect" (Mt. 5:48). Do you see in what [sense] the Lord has given us that which is in His likeness? "For He maketh His sun to rise on the evil and on the good, and sendeth rain on the just and on the unjust" (Mt. 5:45). If you become an adversary of evil, without malice and forgetful of your aversion to vigil, if you love your brothers and are compassionate, you resemble God. If you pardon your enemy from the heart, you resemble God. If your attitude towards the brother who has offended you resembles that of God towards you, a sinner, by mercy towards your neighbor you resemble God. Thus you possess that which is in the image, because you are endowed with reason, but you would become in the likeness in acquiring goodness. Acquire "bowels of mercies and kindness" (Col. 3:12) that you may put on Christ (cf. Gal. 3:27). For those things through which you acquire compassion are the same as those through which you put on Christ, and intimacy with Him makes you close to God.

Thus this history (in Genesis) is an education in human life. "Let Us make man according to Our image." He possessed that which is in the image by the creation; let him also become that which is in the likeness. God has given him this potential; if He had also created you according to the likeness, where would be your privilege? Through what have you been crowned? And if the Creator had given everything to you, how would the kingdom of heaven open itself for you? But one part is given to you, while the other is left unfinished; it is for you to finish yourself that you may become worthy of the reward which comes from God.

Ibid., pp. 207-211.

[4] (Text #18). "And God made man, according to the image of God He made Him."

"Man! says the woman, and what about me? It is the male who was created, for, she says, He did not say 'her' who is man, but by the term 'man' He is shown to mean the masculine." But no! in order that nobody, through ignorance, should take the expression "man" (ἄνθρωπος) to refer only to the male, the Scripture has added: "male and female He made them." The woman also possesses, like the male, that which has been created in the image of God. Equally honorable are both their natures, equal their virtues, equal their reward and alike their condemnation. Let her not say, I am weak. Weakness is of the flesh; strength is in the soul.

Since indeed that which is in the image of God possesses the same honor, let the virtue and the manifestation of good works be the same. There is no recourse for one who wants to invoke the excuse of bodily weakness ...

Is the nature of man ever capable of competing with that of the woman who passes her life in privations? Is he capable, he, the man, of imitating

4

the endurance of women in fasting, their zealous labor in prayer, the abundance of their tears, their diligence in good works? ...

You have therefore become like God by goodness, patience, fellowship, by loving others and loving your brothers, by detesting evil and controlling the passions of sin that dominion may be yours. *Ibid.,* pp. 213-217.

[5] (Text #4). Reflect on how you were fashioned. Consider the workshop from which your nature derived. It is by the hand of God that you have received. May what was fashioned by God not be soiled by evil, or altered by sin: do not fall from the hand of God. You are a vessel modelled by God, having come into being from God: glorify your Creator. You have not been created for anything other than to be an instrument appropriate to the glory of God. And this entire universe is for you like a book in which the text publishes the glory of God: the hidden and invisible grandeur of God He announces to you through it - to you who possess a mind capable of comprehending truth. Remember carefully, then, what has been said.

(Text #5). "And God blessed them, saying, Increase and multiply (αὐξάνεσθε καὶ πληθύνεσθε), and fill the earth." There are two kinds of growth: that of the body and that of the soul. Now the growth of the soul is progress toward perfection through what is learned; the growth of the body is the evolution* from smallness to normal stature.

Now, "grow" is said of animals devoid of reason, in reference to bodily maturity, in the sense of the realization of nature, but to us is said 'grow' according to the interior man, with reference to the progress leading to God. So Paul did in "forgetting those things which are behind and reaching forth unto those things which are before" (Phil 3:13). Such is growth in spiritual things, the acquisition of piety, the stretching out toward the better, when we incline without ceasing towards the things that are, always leave behind those acquired before, and seek, as much as is necessary, that which is still lacking in piety ...

Grow, then, with the growth according to God, with the perfecting of the inner man.

Ibid. Homily II, pp. 235-237.

2. St. Symeon the New Theologian:
[6] God, in the beginning, before He planted Paradise and gave it over to the first-created ones, in five days set in order the earth and what is on it, and the heaven and what is in it. And on the sixth day He created Adam and placed him as lord and king of the whole visible creation. Then there was not yet Paradise. But this world was from God as a kind of Paradise,

---

*ἀποκατάστασις - St. Basil's sole usage of this term: here in the sense of evolution, according to G. W. F. Lampe *A Patristic Greek Lexicon* 1965.

although it was material and sensuous. God gave it over to the authority of Adam and all his descendents, as the divine Scripture says ...Do you see how God gave over to man at the beginning this whole world as a kind of Paradise? ...

Do you see how everything visible which is on the earth, and that is in the sea - everything God gave over into the authority of Adam and his descendents? For what He said to Adam He said to all of us, just as to the Apostles He said, "What I say unto you I say unto all" (Mk. 13:37), because He knew that our race was to increase and that there was to be an innumerable multitude of men.

If now, after we transgressed the commandment and were condemned to die, people have so multiplied, then just imagine how many there would have been if all those born from the creation of the world had not died! And what kind of life they would have lived, being immortal and incorrupt, strangers to sin, sorrows, cares, and difficult necessities! And how, prospering in the keeping of the commandments and the good ordering of the dispositions of the heart, in time they would have ascended into the most perfect glory, and being changed, would have drawn near to God; and the soul of each one would have become light-bearing by reason of the illuminations which would have been poured out upon it from the Divinity! And this sensuous and crudely material body would have become as it were immaterial and spiritual, above all senses; and the joy and rejoicing with which we then would have been filled by fellowship one with the other, in truth would have been unutterable and beyond human thought.

The Sin of Adam, Homily 45, pp. 64-65. © St. Herman of Alaska Brotherhood, Platina, CA 1979.

3. St. John Chrysostom:

[7] O woman, what have you done? ...Why did you disgrace yourself, departing from the one for whom you were created, as whose helpmate you were made, in whose dignity you had equal share, one with him in being and one in language?

Homily 16 (12), CUA, p. 214.

[8] "Your yearning will be for your husband, and he will be your master." As if to explain His reasons to the woman, the loving God said this, meaning, In the beginning I created you equal in esteem to your husband, and my intention was that in everything you would share with him as an equal, and as I entrusted control of everything to your husband, so did I to you; but you abused your equality of status.

Homily 17 (36), Ibid., p. 240.

[9] "Let us make man, according to Our image and likeness," he did not stop there, but through the following verse made clear to us what was the reason for choosing the word "image." What in fact does the text go on to say? "Let them have dominion over the fish of the sea, the flying creatures of heaven ..." So "image" refers to the matter of control, not anything else, in other words, God created the human being as having control of everything on earth, and nothing on earth is greater than the human being, under whose authority everything falls.
Hom. 10 (9), Ib., p. 110.

[10] The human being is the creature more important than all the other visible beings, and for this creature all the others have been produced (prior to man).
Hom. 8 (4, 5), Ib., p. 107.
[11] So who is this to whom He says, 'Let us make man'? (Christ).
Hom. 8 (8), Ib., p. 109.

4. St. Diadochos of Photiki:
[12] Our likeness to God requires our cooperation. When the intellect begins to perceive the Holy Spirit with full consciousness, we should realize that grace is beginning to paint the divine likeness over the divine image in us. If the intellect does not receive the perfection of the divine likeness through such illumination, although it may have almost every other virtue, it will still have no share in perfect love.
On Spiritiual Knowledge, Text 89, *Philokalia*, Vol. 1, p. 288.

5. St. Didymus the Blind:*
[13] "Man" signifies both the composite living being consisting of a soul and a body, and more particularly the soul. Peter, the chief of the apostles, calls the soul "the hidden man of the heart" (1 Pet. 3:4). Likewise the blessed Paul: "I delight in the law of God after the inward man" (Rom. 7:22), that is, according to the mind, the soul ...
The blessed Paul does not use the designation "man" only for the composite, but he also extends its meaning to include its visible and perceptible part, that is, the body, when he says: "Though our outward man perish, yet the inward man is renewed day by day" (2 Cor. 4:16).

---

*Note: The ideas which Didymus derived from Origen regarding the pre-existence of souls and related conclusions were condemned in the Fifth Ecumenical Council held in Constantinople in 553 A.D., according to the Pedalion [The Rudder] compiled by Saints Nicodemus and Agapius. He was, however, greatly respected in his time as head of the catechetical school of Alexandria in the latter part of the fourth century A.D. Despite the loss of his sight at the age of 4, he acquired great erudition, was visited by St. Anthony the Great whenever he came to Alexandria, and is listed in the Prologue on October 18.

At first thought, each of us is composed of a soul and a body, but there are some who say that man is constituted of three parts: the soul, the body and the spirit. They also base their opinion on a text of the Apostle: "the God of peace sanctify you wholly; and I pray God your whole spirit and soul and body be preserved [integrated] blameless" (1 Thess. 5:23), considering that it would not follow that it is said of the Holy Spirit that He should be integrated, since He has never grown weak. They have given as proof this other saying: "the Spirit Himself beareth witness with our spirit" (Rom. 8:16). Our spirit, they say, is something other than the Holy Spirit, since it receives the Holy Spirit's witness when it is well disposed ...

We have said that man - that is principally the intellect or soul - is that which participates in God, becoming by this very participation His image, just as we say that whoever participates in virtue is the image of virtue. Paul indeed understood this, he who spoke in Christ, saying to those he exhorted to make themselves images of Christ "until Christ be formed in you" (Gal. 4:16), teaching also the true understanding concerning Christ, which comes within the soul, imprints it with His characteristics and makes it into His image.

Sur la Genèse, IV 6, 9, 10, Vol. 1, pp. 141-143, 149. © Sources Chrétiennes No. 233, Les Éditions du Cerf, Paris 1976.

But it is necessary to examine the words "And God made man ...male and female He made them." Why when the order of God concerned a single human being, does the associated phrase say: "created He them?" According to the literal sense, one can say that we have here the proof that woman is consubstantial with man: both are comprised in the same species, and because of this it says: "Let us make man." The words "male and female" indicate, on the contrary, the distinction which God has provided between them with a view to descendance; they show at the same time that indeed woman is also "in the image of God": that both have the same capacities: those of imitating God, of participating in the Holy Spirit and of acquiring virtue.

And since we say that the term "man" is also a name for mind and soul, let us understand the anagogical sense of the words "male and female": the teaching power capable of putting the seed of the Word within souls capable of receiving it should be called "male;" and those symbolically have the "female" place who cannot give birth to anything from themselves but receive education from others as a kind of seed. And on the sense-perceptible level the female and the male are made by God, but on the spiritual level each person for himself and by his own choice occupies the place of the teacher, who is male and is the sower of good things, or else becomes the disciple receiving seed from another and attains the female...

Ibid., pp. 158-160.

"And God blessed them," in that they were going to consummate the marriage and were at the point of starting the descendance of humanity, for He also added: "Increase and multiply," indicating that procreation and what is needed to achieve it are free of prohibition or hindrance, because in this way they were to become the parents of those descended from them, who according to the commandment of God, were to fill the earth. For He said: "Fill the earth."
Ibid., IV, 14, 15; V, 1, pp. 159, 165.

6. St. Gregory of Nyssa:
[14] Man and woman are a departure from the prototype, for "In Christ Jesus there is neither male nor female" (Gal. 3:28). Thus the creation of our nature is in a sense twofold: one made like God, one divided according to this distinction.
[15] What difference do we discern between the Divine and that which has been made like the Divine? ...The former is uncreate, while the latter has its being from creation ... Uncreated nature is also immutable ...while the created nature cannot exist without change; for its very passage from non-existence to existence is a certain motion and change.
On the Making of Man, XVI (7, 12) p. 405. NPNF SS Vol. V, Wm B. Eerdmans Publishing Co., Grand Rapids MI 1976.

[16] If procreation is after sin, how would souls have come into being if the first of mankind had remained sinless? ...(cf. Luke 20:35, 36 re Sadducees) "In the resurrection they neither marry, nor are given in marriage; neither can they die any more, for they are equal to the angels, and are the children of God, being the children of the resurrection." Now the resurrection promises us nothing else than the restoration of the fallen to their ancient state; for the grace we look for is a certain return to the first life, to bring back again to Paradise him who was cast out from it ...It is clear that the life before the transgression was a kind of angelic life ...Yet while, as has been said, there is no marriage among them, the armies of the angels are in countless myriads; for so Daniel declared in his visions: so, in the same way, if there had not come upon us as a result of sin a change for the worse, and removal from equality with the angels, neither should we have needed marriage that we might multiply; but whatever the mode of increase in the angelic nature is (unspeakable and inconceivable by human conjectures, except that it assuredly exists [countless myriads, being one essence, and at the same time numerically many]), it would have operated also in the case of men, who were 'made a little lower than the angels' (Ps. 8:6), to increase mankind to the measure determined by its Maker ...
Since He saw beforehand by His all-seeing power the failure of their will to keep a direct course to what is good, and its consequent declension

from the angelic life, in order that the multitude of human souls might not be cut short by its fall from that mode by which the angels were increased and multiplied, - for this reason, I say, He formed for our nature that contrivance for increase which befits those who had fallen into sin, implanting in mankind, instead of the angelic majesty of nature, that animal and irrational mode by which they now succeed one another.

Hence ...the great David pitying the misery of man mourns over his nature with such words as these, that 'man being in honor knew it not' ...'he is compared to the beasts that have no understanding and made like unto them' (Ps. 49 [50]:13). For he truly was made like the beasts, who received in his nature the present mode of transient generation, on account of his inclination to material things.

Ibid.,XVII (1-5) pp. 406-407.

[17] These attributes, then, human nature took to itself from the side of the brutes; for those qualities with which brute life was armed for self-preservation, when transferred to human life, became passions ...if reason instead assumes sway over such emotions, each of them is transmuted to a form of virtue: for anger produces courage, terror caution, fear obedience, hatred aversion from vice, the power of love the desire for what is truly beautiful; high spirit in our character raises our thought above the passions, and keeps it from bondage to what is base.

Ibid., XVIII (1-5), pp. 407-408.

7. St. Athanasius of Alexandria:

[18] The Apostle did not number individually, so as to say "whether Angel, or Throne, or Dominion, or Authority," but he mentions together all according to their kinds, "whether Angels, or Archangels, or Principalities": for in this way is the origination of the creatures ...For so we find it to be in their case, that at once they came to be, with neither first nor second, and they differ from each other in glory ...all praising and standing in service before the Lord.

Discourse II Against the Arians, #49, NPNF SS Vol. IV, p. 375.

8. Psalm 32 [33]:6.

[19] By the word of the Lord the heavens were established; and all the host of them by the breath of his mouth.

9. St. Augustine of Hippo:

[20] The holy angels, whose equals we shall be after the resurrection, if to the end we hold to Christ our Way, always behold the face of God and rejoice in His Word, the only-begotten Son, equal to the Father; and in them first of all wisdom was created. They, therefore, without any doubt

know all creation, of which they are the creatures first made, and they have this knowledge first in the Word of God Himself, in whom are the eternal reasons of all things made in time ...

The knowledge angels have does not remain fixed in a creature without their immediately referring it to the praise and love of Him ...For if the angels turned to themselves or took delight more in themselves than in Him in union with whom they are happy, they would fall swollen with pride. This is what happened with the Devil.

The Literal Meaning of Genesis, Book Four, Ch. 24, ACW, p. 132.

10. St. Basil the Great:

[21] The soul deteriorated when it was perverted from its natural state. What was the soul's supreme good? Attachment to God and conjunction with Him through love. When it failed in this, the soul deteriorated because of weaknesses of many various kinds. But why was it at all capable of evil? Because of its self-determined impulse, an endowment specially appropriate to rational nature. Free from all constraint and endowed by the Creator with self-determining life, because made in God's image ...it had the right and power to preserve its natural state of life, by persevering in the contemplation of the good, and the enjoyment of spiritual pleasure. It had also the power to turn away from the good. And this it is what happened when, sated with this blessed delight, and weighed down as it were with drowsiness, it slipped from the higher sphere, and was mingled with the flesh, for the sake of the enjoyment of base satisfactions.

Homily 9 (5), translated by Henry Bettenson in *The Later Christian Fathers*, Oxford University Press, Oxford 1970, p. 61.

[22] Cattle have their heads bent towards the earth. "Thy head, O man, is turned towards heaven ...'Seek those things which are above'".

Hexaemeron, NPNF, SS Vol. VIII, p. 102.

11. St. Maximus the Confessor

[23] As man I deliberately transgressed the divine commandment, when the devil, enticing me into hope of divinity dragged me down from my natural stability into the realm of sensual pleasure; and he was proud to have brought death into existence, for he delights in the corruption of human nature. Because of this God became perfect man, taking on everything that belongs to human nature except sin (cf. Heb. 4:15); and indeed sin is not part of human nature.

Various Texts on Theology. First Century, #11, *Philokalia,* Vol. 2.

11

THE LAMENT OF EVE

GENESIS, CHAPTER 2 - Selected Verses (Septuagint)

[24] *2:7: And God formed the man of dust of the earth, and breathed upon his face the breath of life, and the man became a living soul.* [1]

2:8: And God planted a garden eastward in Edem [Eden], and placed there the man whom He had formed.

2:9: And God made to spring up also out of the earth every tree beautiful to the eye and good for food, and the tree of life in the midst of the garden, and the tree of learning the knowledge of good and evil. [1]

2:10: And a river proceeds out of Edem ...

2:15: And the Lord took the man whom He had formed, and placed him in the garden of Delight, to cultivate and keep it. [2]

2:16: And the Lord gave a charge to Adam, saying, Of every tree which is in the garden thou mayest freely eat,

2:17: but of the tree of knowledge of good and evil - of it ye shall not eat, but in whatever day ye eat of it, ye shall surely die. [3]

2:18: And the Lord God said, It is not good that the man should be alone, Let Us make for him a help suitable to him. [1, 4, 5]

2:19: And God formed yet farther out of the earth all the wild beasts of the field, and all the birds of the sky, and he brought them to Adam, to see what he would call them, and whatever Adam called any living creature, that was the name of it. [6]

2:20 And Adam gave names to all the cattle and to all the birds of the sky, and to all the wild beasts of the field, but for Adam there was not found a help like to himself.

2:21: And God brought a trance upon Adam, and he slept, and he took one of his ribs, and filled up the flesh instead thereof.

2:22: And God formed the rib which He took from Adam into a woman, because she was taken out of her husband.

2:23: And Adam said, This now is bone of my bones, and flesh of my flesh; she shall be called woman, because she was taken out of her husband.

2:24: Therefore shall a man leave his father and his mother and shall cleave to his wife, and they two shall be one flesh. [7]

PROLOGUE - THE STORY OF EVE

The Fathers on Genesis 2

1. St. John of Damascus:

[25] All that is produced is also subject to change. For those things must be subject to change whose production has its origin in change. And change consists in being brought into being out of nothing, and in transforming a substratum of matter into something different. Inanimate things, then, and things without reason undergo bodily changes, while the changes of things endowed with reason depend on choice. For reason consists of a speculative and a practical part. The speculative part is the contemplation of the nature of things, and the practical consists of deliberation and defines the true reason for what is to be done. The speculative side is called mind or wisdom, and the practical side is called reason or prudence. Everyone, then, who deliberates does so in the belief that the choice of what is to be done lies in his hands, that he may choose what seems best as the result of his deliberation, and having chosen may act upon it. And if this is so, free will must necessarily be very closely related to reason. For either man is an irrational being, or, if he is rational, he is master of his acts and endowed with free will. Hence also creatures without reason do not enjoy free will: for nature leads them rather than they nature, and so they do not oppose the natural appetite, but as soon as their appetite longs after anything they rush headlong after it. But man, being rational, leads nature rather than nature him, and so when he desires anything he has the power to curb his appetite or to indulge it as he pleases. Hence also creatures devoid of reason are the subjects neither of praise nor blame, while man is the subject of both praise and blame.

Note also that the angels, being rational, are endowed with free will, and, inasmuch as they are created, are liable to change. This in fact is made plain by the devil who, although made good by the Creator, became of his own free will the inventor of evil.

Exposition of the Orthodox Faith, Chap. XXVII; NPNF Vol. IX SS, p. 40-41.

[26] We ought to understand that while God knows all things beforehand, yet He does not predetermine all things. For He knows beforehand those things that are in our power, but He does not predetermine them. For it is not His will that there should be wickedness nor does He choose to compel virtue. So that predetermination is the work of the divine command based on fore-knowledge. But on the other hand God predetermines those things which are not within our power in accordance with His prescience. For already God in His prescience has pre-judged all things in accordance with His goodness and justice. Bear in mind, too, that

virtue is a gift from God implanted in our nature, and that He Himself is the source and cause of all good, and without His cooperation and help we cannot will or do any good thing ...

[27] But since God in His prescience knew that man would transgress and become liable to destruction, He made from him a female to be a help to him like himself; a help, indeed, for the conservation of the race after the transgression from age to age by generation. For the earliest formation is called 'making' and not 'generation.' For 'making' is the original formation at God's hands, while 'generation' is the succession from each other made necessary by the sentence of death imposed upon us on account of the transgression.

[28] This man He placed in Paradise, a home that was alike spiritual and sensible. For he lived in the body on the earth in the realm of sense, while he dwelt in the spirit among the angels, cultivating divine thoughts, and being supported by them: living in naked simplicity a life free from artificiality, and being led up through His creations to the one and only Creator, in whose contemplation he found joy and gladness.

[29] When therefore He had furnished his nature with free will, He imposed a law on him, not to taste of the tree of knowledge ...And with this command He gave the promise that, if he should preserve the dignity of the soul by giving the victory to reason, and acknowledging his Creator and observing His command, he should share eternal blessedness and live to all eternity, proving mightier than death. But if he should subject the soul to the body, comparing himself in ignorance of his true dignity to the senseless beasts, and shaking off his Creator's yoke, and neglecting His divine injunction, he will be liable to death and corruption, and will be compelled to labor throughout a miserable life. For it was no profit to man to obtain incorruption while still untried and unproved, lest he should fall into pride and under judgment of the devil ...

[30] It was necessary, therefore, that man should first be put to the test ...For being intermediate between God and matter, he was destined, if he kept the command, to be delivered from his natural relation to existing things and to be made one with God's estate, and to be immovably established in goodness, but, if he transgressed and inclined rather to what was material, and tore his mind from the Author of his being, I mean God, his fate was to be corruption, and he was to become subject to passion instead of passionless, and mortal instead of immortal, and dependent on connection and unsettled generation. And in his desire for life he would cling to pleasures as though they were necessary to maintain it, and would fearlessly abhor those who sought to deprive him of these, and transfer his desire from God to matter, and his anger from the real enemy of his salvation to his own brethren.

Ibid., Chap. XXX, pp. 42-43.

14

[31] God planted the tree of life and the tree of knowledge. The tree of knowledge was for trial, and proof, and exercise of man's obedience and disobedience: and hence it was named the tree of the knowledge of good and evil, or else it was because to those who partook of it was given power to know their own nature. Now this is a good thing for those who are mature, but an evil thing for the immature and those whose appetites are too strong ...

[32] God meant that we should be thus free from passion ...He meant us further to be free from care and to have but one work to perform, to sing as do the angels, without ceasing or intermission, the praises of the Creator, and to delight in contemplation of Him and to cast all our care on Him. This is what the Prophet David proclaimed to us when he said, "Cast thy burden on the Lord, and He will sustain thee (Ps. 54:22). And, again in the Gospels, Christ taught His disciples, saying, "Take no thought for your life, what ye shall eat, nor for your body what ye shall put on" (Mt. 6:25). And further, "Seek ye first the Kingdom of God and His righteousness and all these things shall be added unto you" (Ibid., 33) ...

The tree of life, on the other hand, was a tree having the energy that is the cause of life, or to be eaten only by those who deserve to live and are not subject to death.

Ibid., Chap XI, p. 29.

[33] Providence, then, is the care that God takes over existing things. And again: Providence is the will of God through which all existing things receive their fitting issue ...God is both Creator and Provider, and His creative and preserving and providing power is simply His good will. For "whatsoever the Lord pleased that did He in heaven and in earth" (Job 1:11).

Ibid., Chap. XXIX, p. 41.

2. St. Symeon the New Theologian:

[34] Inasmuch as human nature lost its blessed state through the transgression of Adam, it is essential for us to know what Adam was before the loss of the blessed state, and in what consisted this blessed state, or that good and divine condition which man had before the transgression. The Holy Fathers tell us that God became man in order that through His becoming man He might again raise up human nature into the blessed state. Therefore, we must know in what way it is that man, through the Economy of Christ's Incarnation, may again come into the blessed state.

[35] God, in the beginning when He created man, created him holy, passionless and sinless, in His own image and likeness. And man was then precisely like God who created him; for the holy, sinless and passionless God creates also His creatures holy, passionless and sinless. But inasmuch as unalterability and unchangingness are characteristic of the Unoriginate

and Uncreated Divinity alone, therefore the created man naturally was alterable and changeable, although he had the means and the possibility, with the help of God, not to be subject to alteration and change.

[36] Thus man was holy, and as holy he had no need of any law; for the righteous need no law. What need is there of the law for one who is holy, passionless and pure? The law commands to do good and not to do evil. But the Scripture says that "God saw everything that He had made, and behold, it was very good" (Gen. 1:31) ...

[37] However, inasmuch as it was in his power to eat of every tree of Paradise and from the very Tree of Life itself, there was given to him a commandment not to eat from one tree only, so that he might know that he was alterable and changeable, and might beware, and might always remain in that good and divine condition. God, by those words which He said to him in giving the commandment that if he should eat he would die, gave him to understand that he was alterable and changeable.

The Sin of Adam, Homily 2, pp. 40-41.

3. St. John Chrysostom:

[38] Why was it called the tree of the knowledge of good and evil? There are, you see, many people bent on controversy who endeavor to maintain that after eating from the tree Adam had knowledge to discriminate between good and evil - an opinion of the utmost absurdity ...Earlier we dealt with many aspects of the intelligence granted the human being by God, demonstrating it from the imposition of names which he [Adam] gave to all animals, the birds and the brute beasts, and the fact that he was endowed with prophetic grace (cf. Gen. 2:24) along with this ineffable intelligence lest anyone come up with such an opinion ...How could he have been ignorant of what is good and what is evil? ...How, after all, could an ignorant person be commanded that transgression is wrong? This, however, is not the case - perish the thought; on the contrary, he knew quite well. It was, after all, on that account that God from the outset equipped this creature with independence: if this had not been the case, he ought not to have been punished when he broke the command nor considered worthy of praise for keeping it. You see, the fact that he fell under death's sway on account of the fall is clear both from the command itself and from what happened later. Listen, in fact, to the woman in person speaking to the serpent: "From fruit of the tree in the middle of the garden," God said, "You are not to eat, lest you die." It follows that before eating they were in fact not subject to death; if this were not the case, he would not have imposed death on them by way of penalty after the eating ...

[39] Since, however, he was guilty of great inadvertence and together with his wife fell into this disaster through transgression of the command given him by tasting of the tree, accordingly it was called the tree of the

16

knowledge of good and evil - not because he was ignorant of good and evil before this ...but because after eating it they were divested of the glory from above and also had experience of their obvious nakedness ...in connection with it there took place the contest, as you might say, between obedience and disobedience.

Homily 16 (16, 18), CUA Vol. 74, p. 218, 220.

4. St. Gregory of Nazianzus:

[40] I have heard the Scripture say: Who can find a valiant woman? (cf. Prov. 31:10) and declare that she is a divine gift, and that a good marriage is brought about by the Lord. Even those without are of the same mind if they say that a man can win no fairer prize than a good wife, nor a worse one than her opposite ...

She indeed who was given to Adam as a helpmate for him, because it was not good for man to be alone, instead of an assistant became an enemy, and instead of a fellow laborer, an opponent, and beguiling the man by means of pleasure, estranged him through the tree of knowledge from the tree of life.

[41] But she who was given by God to my father became not only, as is less wonderful, his assistant, but even his leader, drawing him on by her influence in deed and word to the highest intelligence; judging it best in all other respects to be overruled by her husband according to the law of marriage, but not being ashamed, in regard of piety, even to offer herself as his teacher. Admirable indeed as was this conduct of hers, it was still more admirable that he should readily acquiesce in it. She is a woman who while others have been honored and extolled for natural and artificial beauty, has acknowledged but one kind of beauty, that of the soul, and the preservation, or the restoration as far as possible, of the Divine image. Pigments and devices for adornment she has rejected as worthy of women on the stage. The only genuine form of noble birth she recognized is piety, and the knowledge of whence we are sprung and whither we are tending. The only safe and inviolable form of wealth is, she considered, to strip oneself of wealth for God and the poor, and especially for those of our own kin who are unfortunate; and such help only as is necessary, she held to be rather a reminder, than a relief of their distress, while a more liberal beneficence brings stable honor and most perfect consolation. Some women have excelled in thrifty management, others in piety, while she, difficult as it is to unite the two virtues, has surpassed all in both of them, both by her eminence in each, and by the fact that she alone has combined them together ...She applied herself to God and Divine things as closely as if absolutely released from household cares, allowing neither branch of her duty to interfere with the other, but rather making each of them support the other.

17

[42] What time or place for prayer ever escaped her? To this she was drawn before all other things in the day, or rather, who had such hope of receiving an immediate answer to her requests? Who paid such reverence to the hand and countenance of the priests? Or honored all kinds of philosophy? Who reduced the flesh by more constant fast and vigil? Or stood like a pillar at the night-long and daily psalmody? Who had a greater love for virginity, though patient of the marriage bond herself? Who was a better patron of the orphan and the widow? Who aided as much in the alleviation of the misfortunes of the mourner? These things, small as they are, and perhaps contemptible in the eyes of some, because not easily attainable by most people (for that which is unattainable comes, through envy, to be thought not even credible), are in my eyes most honorable, since they were the discoveries of her faith and the undertakings of her spiritual fervor. So also in the holy assemblies, or places, her voice was never to be heard except in the necessary responses of the service.

Oration XVIII. On the Death of His Father (7, 8, 9). NPNF, Vol. VII SS, p. 256-257.

[42A] This being He placed in Paradise, whatever the Paradise may have been, having honored him with the gift of free will (in order that God might belong to him as the result of his choice, no less than to Him who had implanted the seeds of it), to till the immortal plants, by which is meant perhaps the divine conceptions, both the simpler and the more perfect; naked in his simplicity and unartificial life, and without any covering or screen; for it was fitting that he who was from the beginning should be such. Also He gave him a law, as a material for his free will to act upon. This law was a commandment as to what plants he might partake of, and which one he might not touch. This latter was the Tree of Knowledge; not however, because it was evil from the beginning when planted; nor was it forbidden because God grudged it to us ...But it would have been good if partaken of at the proper time, for the tree was, according to my theory, Contemplation, upon which it is only safe for those who have reached maturity of habit to enter; but which is not good for those who are still somewhat simple and greedy in their habit; just as solid food is not good for those who are yet tender, and have need of milk.

Oration XXXVIII On the Theophany, or Birthday of Christ (11), Ib. p. 348.

5. St. John Chrysostom:

[43] "Therefore, just as the church is subject to Christ, so let the wives be to their own husbands in everything. Husbands, love your wives, just as Christ also loved the church and gave Himself for it" (Eph. 5:24-25). Let there be an interchange of service and submission. For then there will be

no such thing as slavish service ...It would be better if both masters and slaves were servants to one another - for it is better to be a slave in this way than free in any other. Imagine the case of a man having a hundred slaves and in no way serving them; and suppose again a different case, of a hundred friends, all waiting on one another. Which will lead the happier life?

Homily XIX on Ephesians V. NPNF, Vol. XIII, p. 142.

6. St. Athanasius of Alexandria:

[44] But turn back they can, if they ...have got rid of all foreign matter that has affected their soul, and can show it in the simplicity as it was made, that so they may be able by it to behold the Word of the Father, after whose likeness they were originally made ...Then surely ...being thoroughly brightened, the soul beholds as in a mirror the image of the Father, whose image the Savior is ...It is further possible to attain to the knowledge of God from the things which are seen, since Creation, as though in written characters, declares in a loud voice, by its order and harmony, its own Lord and Creator, "for the invisible things of Him since the creation of the world are clearly seen, being understood by the things that are made" (Rom. 1:20).

Against the Heathen, Part II (34). NPNF, Vol. IV SS, p. 22.

7. Bishop Nikolai Velimirovich:

[45] It is God's will that the human race increase. The means by which it does so are of divine artistry; how a man may leave his father and his mother and cleave to his wife is a divine mystery. To leave one's parents does not mean to abandon them, but rather to become a parent oneself. When children become parents, they are no longer merely children to their parents, but also their friends. When married sons come to know the mystery and suffering of procreation, they respect their parents still more. The marriage bond never frees a man from respecting and obeying his parents. The original commandment of God to honor one's parents must be fulfilled. But, in the normal course of things, a man leaves his parents and, becoming a parent himself, becomes a founder of a new future; and his parents, who have fulfilled their role in the world, depart. However, the leaving of one's parents does not consist in this alone. In some unfathonable mystery, a man cleaves to his wife and detaches himself from his parents. Theodoret says: 'Christ Himself, having left His Father on high, united Himself to the Church.'

The Prologue from Ochrid, May 28th, Vol. 2, p. 233. Lazarica Press, Birmingham 1986.

THE LAMENT OF EVE

GENESIS, CHAPTER 3 - (Septuagint)

[46] *3:1: And the two were naked, both Adam and his wife, and were not ashamed.* [1]

3:2: Now the serpent was the most crafty of all the brutes on the earth, which the Lord God made, and the serpent said to the woman, Wherefore has God said, Eat not of every tree of the garden? [1]

3:3: And the woman said to the serpent, We may eat of the fruit of the trees of the garden, [1]

3:4: but of the fruit of the tree which is in the midst of the garden, God said, Ye shall not eat of it, neither shall ye touch it, lest ye die. [1]

3:5: And the serpent said to the woman, Ye shall not surely die. [1,2]

3:6: For God knew that in whatever day ye should eat of it your eyes would be opened, and ye would be as gods, knowing good and evil. [1]

3:7: And the woman saw that the tree was good for food, and that it was pleasant to the eyes to look upon and beautiful to contemplate, and having taken of its fruit she ate, and she gave to her husband also with her, and they ate. [1,2]

3:8: And the eyes of both were opened, and they perceived that they were naked, and they sewed fig leaves together, and made themselves aprons to go round them. [1]

3:9: And they heard the voice of the Lord God walking in the garden in the afternoon; and both Adam and his wife hid themselves from the face of the Lord God in the midst of the trees of the garden. [3,4]

3:10: And the Lord God called Adam and said to him, Adam, where art thou?

3:11: And he said to Him, I heard Thy voice as Thou walkedst in the garden, and I feared because I was naked and I hid myself.

3:12: And God said to him, Who told thee that thou wast naked, unless thou hast eaten of the tree concerning which I charged thee of it alone not to eat? [4]

3:13: And Adam said, The woman whom Thou gavest to be with me -- she gave me of the tree and I ate. [6]

3:14: And the Lord God said to the woman, Why hast thou done this? And the woman said, The serpent deceived me and I ate. [6,8]

3:15: And the Lord God said to the serpent, Because thou hast done this thou art cursed above all cattle and all the brutes of the earth, on thy breast and belly thou shalt go, and thou shalt eat earth all the days of thy life.

3:16: And I will put enmity between thee and the woman and between thy seed and her seed, he shall watch against thy head, and thou shalt watch against his heel.

3:17: And to the woman He said, I will greatly multiply thy pains and thy groanings; in pain thou shalt bring forth children, and thy submission shall be to thy husband, and he shall rule over thee. [6]

3:18: And to Adam He said, Because thou hast hearkened to the voice of thy wife, and eaten of the tree concerning which I charged thee of it only not to eat -- of that thou hast eaten, cursed is the ground in thy labours, in pain shalt thou eat of it all the days of thy life. [8]

3:19: Thorns and thistles shall it bring forth to thee, and thou shalt eat the herb of the field.

3:20: In the sweat of thy face shalt thou eat thy bread until thou return to the earth out of which thou wast taken, for earth thou art and to earth thou shalt return. [6]

3:21: And Adam called the name of his wife Life, because she was the mother of all living. [6]

3:22: And the Lord God made for Adam and his wife garments of skin, and clothed them. [6]

3:23: And God said, Behold, Adam is become as one of us, to know good and evil, and now lest at any time he stretch forth his hand, and take of the tree of life and eat, and so he shall live for ever - - [3, 6]

3:24: So the Lord God sent him forth out of the garden of Delight to cultivate the ground out of which he was taken.

3:25: And He cast out Adam and caused him to dwell over against the garden of Delight, and stationed the cherubs and the fiery sword that turns about to keep the way of the tree of life. [6, 7, 10]

The Fathers on Genesis 3

1. St. John Chrysostom:
[47] "They were both naked, Adam and his wife, without feeling shame." Consider, I ask you, the transcendence of their blessed condition, how they were superior to all bodily concerns, how they lived on earth as if they were in heaven, and though in fact possessing a body they did not feel the limitations of their bodies. After all, they had no need of shelter or habitation, clothing or anything of that kind. It was not idly or to no purpose that Sacred Scripture indicated this to us; it was that we might learn of this carefree condition of theirs, their trouble-free life and angelic condition, as you might say, and that we might attribute it completely to their indifference when later we see them bereft of all these advantages and, as it were, reduced to the utmost indigence after the great abundance of their wealth.
Homily 16 on Genesis (2). CUA, Vol. 74, pp. 207-209.

[48] Consider from this, dearly beloved, how in the beginning none of the wild beasts then existing caused fear either to the man or to the woman; on the contrary, they recognized human direction and dominion, and as

21

with tame animals these days, so then even the wild and savage ones proved to be subdued. But perhaps in this case some may raise a difficulty and seek to find out if the wild animals also shared the power of speech. Not so - perish the thought; rather, people, following Scripture, need to consider the fact that the words came from the devil, who was spurred on to this deception by his own ill-will, while this wild animal he employed like some convenient instrument so as to be able to set the bait for his own deception and thus upset the woman first of all, being ever more readily susceptible of deception, and then, through her, man the first-formed.

    Ibid., (4), p. 209.

Through her grave negligence she not only failed to turn away but revealed the whole secret of the Lord's direction, thus casting pearls before swine and fulfilling what was said by Christ: "Don't cast your pearls before swine, lest they trample them underfoot, turn on you and tear you to pieces" (Mt. 7:6), as in fact happened in this case. I mean, she exposed to swine, to that evil beast, that is, to the demon acting through it, the divine pearls; he not only trampled on them and opposed them with his words, but turned and led into the rupture of disobedience not only her but also the first-formed man with her. Such is the evil of idly and casually exposing to all and sundry the divine mysteries.

    Ib., (6), pp. 210-211.

[49] True it is that "evil converse corrupts good behavior" (cf. 1 Cor. 15:33). Why was it, after all, that before that wicked demon's advice she entertained no such idea, had no eye for the tree, nor noticed its attractiveness? Because she feared God's direction and the punishment likely to follow from tasting the fruit; now, however, when she was deceived by this evil creature into thinking that not only would they not come to any harm from this but would even be equal to God, then evidently hope of gaining the promised reward drove her to taste it. Not content to remain within her own proper limits, but considering the enemy and foe of her salvation to be more trustworthy than God's words, she learned shortly afterwards through her own experience the lethal effect of such advice and the disaster brought on them from tasting the fruit ...

[50] Do you see how the devil led her captive, handicapped her reasoning, and caused her to set her thoughts on goals beyond her real capabilities, in order that she might be puffed up with empty hopes and lose her hold on the advantages already accorded her? ...

[51] O woman, what have you done? You have not only followed that deadly counsel literally and trampled on the law imposed on you by God, spurning His instruction and treating it with such displeasure as to be discontented with such great enjoyment, but you have presumed to take fruit

from the one tree which the Lord bade you not to lay hold of, you put faith in the words of the serpent, you regarded its advice worthy of greater heed than the instruction given you by the Creator, and have been ensnared in such awful deception, as to be incapable of any claim to excuse. Surely, you are not, after all, of the same nature as the one who offered you the advice? He happened in fact to be one of those under your control, one of the servants placed by providence under your authority. Such being the case, why did you disgrace yourself, departing from the one for whom you were created, as whose helpmate you were made, in whose dignity you had equal share, one with him in being and one in language - why then did you agree to enter into converse with the serpent, and by means of this creature accept the advice of the devil, which was plainly at variance with the Creator's injunction, without being turned aside from such evil intent, but rather presuming to taste the fruit through hope of what had been promised?

[52] Well and good, then: so you cast yourself into such an abyss and robbed yourself of your pre-eminent dignity. Why did you make your husband a partner in this grievous disaster, why prove to be the temptress of the person whose helpmate you were intended to be, and why for a tiny morsel alienate him along with yourself from the favor of God? ...

[53] Great was the man's indifference, too: even though like him she was human and his wife as well, still he should have kept God's law intact and given it preference before her improper greed, and not joined her as a partner in her fall.

Ib., (10, 11, 12, 13), pp. 213-215.

[54] Once they disobeyed what had been commanded, they were now made to become aware of things that previously they had no awareness of on account of the benevolence of the Lord shown to them. So when you hear that "Their eyes were opened," understand it in the sense that He saw to it that they would now experience their nakedness and the loss of the glory they enjoyed before eating ...God opened the eyes of Hagar (cf. Gen. 21:19), not because she could not see before then but because He awakened her mind ...

From that event knowledge of sin then entered the scene, and shame as well ...

[55] The loving Lord, you see, instructing the human being in the beginning and from the very outset, and wanting to teach him that he has a creator and craftsman who produces all visible realities and shapes him as well, wished to reveal to him his own dominion through this slight command. To make a comparison with a generous master who provides a great home full of wonders for someone's enjoyment: he is prepared to take not the due price but some small part so as in his own interests to protect his title of dominion and to ensure that the person may have precise under-

standing that he is not the owner of the property but enjoys its use out of his grace and beneficence. In just the same way does our Lord entrust everything to the human being, providing him with a way of life in the garden and enjoyment of everything in it; lest he be gradually perverted in his thinking and come to regard visible things as self-sufficient and get inflated ideas of his own importance, He bids him stay away from the one tree, setting a severe penalty for transgression so that he may be aware he is under His dominion and along with everything else is a partaker of His generosity.

Ib., (15, 17, 18), pp. 217, 219-220.

2. St. Gregory of Nazianzus:

[56] Our warfare is directed against that adversary and foe within us, who uses ourselves as his weapons against ourselves, and most fearful of all, hands us over to the death of sin ... But the scope of our art is to provide the soul with wings, to rescue it from the world and give it to God, and to watch over that which is in His image if it abides, to take it by the hand if it is in danger, or restore it if ruined, to make Christ to dwell in the heart by the Spirit: and in short, to deify, and bestow heavenly bliss upon one who belongs to the heavenly host ...

This is why the new was substituted for the old, why He Who suffered was for suffering recalled to life ...This is the reason for the generation and the virgin, for the manger and Bethlehem: the generation on behalf of the creation, the virgin on behalf of the woman, Bethlehem because of Eden ...All these are a training from God for us, and a healing for our weakness, restoring the old Adam to the place whence he fell, and conducting us to the tree of life, from which the tree of knowledge estranged us, when partaken of unseasonably and improperly.

In Defense of His Flight to Pontus (21, 22, 24, 25), NPNF, Vol. VII SS, p. 209, 210.

[57] The woman sinned, and so did Adam. The serpent deceived them both, and one was not found to be the stronger and the other the weaker. But do you consider the better? Christ saves both by His passion. Was He made flesh for the man? So He was also for the woman. Did He die for the man? The woman also is saved by His death. He is called of the seed of David, and so perhaps you think the man is honored; but He is born of a virgin, and this is on the woman's side. "They two shall be one flesh," so let the one flesh have equal honor. And Paul legislates for chastity by His example. How, and in what way? This sacrament is great, he says, "But I speak concerning Christ and the Church" (Eph. 5:32). It is well for the wife to reverence Christ through her husband; and it is well for the husband not to dishonor the Church through his wife. Let the wife, he says, see that she reverence her husband, for so she does Christ; but also he bids the husband

cherish his wife, for so Christ does the Church (cf. Eph. 5:22f). Let us then give further consideration to this saying.

Oration XXXVII (7) On the Words of the Gospel. Ibid., p. 340.

3. St. Didymus the Blind:

[58] One can interpret in another sense the words: "Adam and his wife hid themselves from the face of the Lord God," understanding His "face" to be His only-begotten Son who is in His image and the "imprint of His substance" (cf. Heb. 1:3). For one who has seen Him "has seen the Father" (Jn. 14:9).

They would thus have been required to do all to preserve that which is "according to His image," a condition in which they had been created; in preferring to be transgressors of the commandment, they renounced being illumined by the image of God. And appropriately they took refuge under the tree in the middle of Paradise, which is the tree of the knowledge of good and evil. For one who hides from the face of God in not practicing virtue, but instead, putting on appearances, is hiding himself under hypocrisy. For one who knows good and evil without distinguishing or choosing the good, but deeming himself to be clever, hides himself from God in giving himself the appearance of virtue...

Being the source of goodness, God, even after our failures, calls us anew, not effacing entirely from our mind the knowledge of good, even if we have turned away from virtue through sin. This is what God, at present also does for Adam in calling him although he has hidden himself, saying to him: "Adam, where art thou?" Adam, in fact, had been placed there by God for the purpose of working and guarding Paradise; he had received this place from Him to be his own. Having distanced himself from there by disobedience, it is proper that he should hear from God: "Where art thou?" That the function one occupies is sometimes called a place, is learned from the Acts of the Apostles, when the apostles, wanting to set a disciple in the place of Judas who had betrayed Jesus, sent this prayer up to God: "Thou Lord, which knowest the hearts of men, show which of these two men Thou hast chosen that he may occupy the place of his ministry" (Acts. 1:24-25). And it follows that Adam, having transgressed in the function assigned him by God, should be cast out of the place corresponding to that function; for he was banished from Paradise ...

Moreover, he who has his citizenship in the heavens (cf. Heb. 11:10, 11:16, 12:22) and who has his heart in heaven, because he has his treasure there (cf. Mt. 6:21) and no longer in a place, is coming to be above the world...

[59] In saying "one of us," God is speaking to the angels, as a king to his body guards. It is known through the Scripture that God puts Himself in community with His creatures ...

"And now lest at any time he stretch forth his hand, and take of the tree of life and eat, and so he shall live for ever." Jealousy is excluded from the divine choir [of heavenly beings], for the reason that much more, and supremely, it cannot exist in God. So it is not jealousy that prevents them from taking anew of the tree of life, but they are prevented from taking it in an inappropriate way. Similarly, the Savior warns: "Give not that which is holy unto the dogs, neither cast ye your pearls before swine" (Mt. 7:6).

Sur la Genèse VI, 9-11; VII, 13, 14, pp. 209-213, 259-261.

4. Bishop Nikolai Velimirovich:

[60] Fear is the first fruit of sin. When Adam sinned, he hid from the face of God. When God called to him, he said: "I heard Thy voice ...and I was afraid". Adam did not know fear before he sinned, nor did he hide from the face of God, but on the contrary, always hastened to meet Him. But as soon as he sinned he was afraid.

The Prologue from Ochrid, June 26, translated by Mother Maria, Vol. 2, pp. 363-364. Lazarica Press, Birmingham 1986.

5. St. Symeon the New Theologian:

[61] In considering the sin by which Adam sinned when he was in the glory and enjoyment of Paradise, no one will find that it was done out of necessity or infirmity, or for any good reason at all, but solely out of disdain for the commandment of God, out of the ingratitude and apostasy which Adam showed with relation to God his Creator. Besides, there was given him by God an opportunity for repentance, that he might obtain forgiveness; and this was for the two following reasons: first, because he had not himself devised the evil, but he was deceived and led into error by the counsel of the devil; secondly, because he was clothed with flesh, for Adam as a creature was subject to change, but could not fall into complete apostasy from God, as did the devil and the demons who followed him, who did not have flesh.

[62] Therefore, a great hope for obtaining mercy is left to man now, when he is clothed with that certain natural infirmity which human nature assumed after the fall, and by reason of which he sins.

The Sin of Adam, Homily 10 (1), p. 45.

[63] God gave the first-created ones a commandment, and commanded them not to taste of the tree of knowledge alone; but Adam disdained this commandment of God, not believing the words of the Creator and Master, who said, "In whatever day ye eat of it, ye shall surely die," but respected as more true the word of the evil devil who said, "Ye shall not surely die. But in whatsoever day ye eat of it, ye shall become as gods, knowing good and evil," and he tasted of that tree. Therefore he was im-

mediately stripped of that incorrupt garment and glory, and was clothed in the nakedness of corruption; and seeing himself naked, he hid himself, and sewing together fig leaves he girded himself so as to cover his shame ...

[64] But Adam did not wish to say, "I sinned," but said rather the contrary of this and placed the blame for the transgression upon God who created everything "very good," saying to Him, "The woman whom Thou gavest to be with me, she gave me of the tree and I ate." And after him she also placed the blame upon the serpent, and they did not wish at all to repent and, falling down before the Lord God, beg forgiveness of Him. For this, God banished them from Paradise, as from a royal palace, to live in this world as exiles. At that time also He decreed that a flaming sword should be turned and should guard the entrance into Paradise. And God did not curse Paradise, since it was the image of the future unending life of the eternal Kingdom of Heaven. If it were not for this reason, it would have been fitting to curse it most of all, since within it was performed the transgression of Adam. But God did not do this, but cursed only the whole rest of the earth, which also was corrupt and brought forth everything by itself; and this was in order that Adam might not have any longer a life free from exhausting labors and sweat ...

[65] And thus it was fitting in all justice for the one who had become corruptible and mortal by reason of the transgression of the commandment, to live upon the corruptible earth and be nourished with corruptible food; for since a life without labor and an abundant food which grew by itself had caused him to forget God and the good things which He had given him and to disdain His commandment, he was therefore justly condemned to work the earth in the sweat of labor and in this way receive from it food little by little as from some kind of steward. Do you see how then the earth received the criminal after it had been cursed and had been deprived of its original productivity by which fruits were produced from it by themselves without labor? And why was this? In order that it might be worked by him in sweat and labors and thus give him that little which it grows for his need, for the support of life, and if it will not be worked, to remain fruitless and to grow only thorns and thistles.

[66] Then also all creatures, when they saw that Adam had been banished from Paradise, no longer wished to submit to him, the criminal: the sun did not wish to shine for him, nor did the moon and the other stars wish to show themselves to him; the springs did not wish to gush forth water, and the rivers to continue their course; the air thought no longer to blow so as not to allow Adam, the sinner, to breathe; the beasts and all the other animals of the earth, when they saw that he had been stripped of his first glory, began to despise him, and all immediately were ready to fall upon him. The heaven, in a certain fashion, was about to strive to fall upon him, and the earth did not wish to bear him any longer.

[67] But God, who created everything and made man - what did He do? Knowing before the creation of the world that Adam would transgress His commandment, and having foreordained for him a new life and a re-creation, which things he was to receive in rebirth in Holy Baptism by virtue of the economy of the Incarnation of His only-begotten Son and our God, He restrained all these creatures by His power, and in His compassion and goodness did not allow them immediately to strive against man, and commanded that the creation should remain in submission to him, and having become corrupt, should serve corrupt man for whom it had been created, with the aim that when man again should be renewed and become spiritual, incorrupt and immortal, then also the whole creation, which had been subjected by God to man to serve him, might be delivered from this servitude, might be renewed together with him, and become incorrupt and as it were spiritual. All this the All-Merciful God foreordained before the creation of the world.

Ibid., Homily 45 (2), pp. 67-69.

6. St. John Chrysostom:

[68] He did not stop loving them at that point. Instead, faithful to his own goodness, he is like a loving father who sees his own son through negligence committing things unworthy of his upbringing and being reduced from his eminent position to the utmost depravity: he is stirred to the depths of his being as a father, yet, far from ceasing to care for him, he displays further concern for him in his desire to extricate him gradually from his abasement and return him to his previous position of dignity ...

You see, for proof that the kingdom has been prepared for us if we are willing to give evidence of virtue and follow the laws laid down by Christ, listen further to His words: "Come, blessed of my Father: inherit the kingdom prepared for you from the foundation of the world" (Mt. 25: 34).

Homily 17 on Genesis (2, 25), CUA, Vol. 74, pp. 222, 235.

[69] As if to explain His reasons to the woman ...hence I subject you to your husband ...because you abandoned your equal, who was sharer with you in the same nature and for whom you were created, and you chose to enter into conversation with that evil creature the serpent ...I now subject you to him in future and designate him as your master for you to recognize his lordship, and since you did not know how to rule, learn well how to be ruled ...It is better that you be subject to him and fall under his lordship than that enjoying freedom and authority, you would be cast into the abyss.

...Let men give good heed, let women give good heed - the former, that they may have nothing to do with those people advising evil actions, and the latter, that that they may advise nothing of the sort.

Ibid., (36, 38), pp. 240-242.

[70] My intention in bringing you into the world, He is saying, was that you should live your life without pain or toil, difficulty or sweat, and that you should be in a state of enjoyment and prosperity, and not subject to the needs of the body but be free from all such and have the good fortune to experience complete freedom. Since, however, such indulgence was of no benefit to you, accordingly I curse the ground so that it will not in future yield its harvest as before without tilling and ploughing; instead I invest you with great labor, toil and difficulty, and with unremitting pain and despair, and I am ensuring that everything you do is achieved only by sweat so that under pressure from these you may have continual guidance in keeping to limits and recognizing your own make-up ...You will endure this as long as the span of your life is extended and you decompose into the material from which you were formed ...

[71] At this point, however, a further question arises for us ...God said, the text tells us. "On the day you eat from it ye shall surely die", yet they are shown living for a great number of years after the disobedience and tasting the food. This seems to pose a problem for those who read the subject matter superficially; if however you give your attention to it in the proper spirit, the verse is clear and offers no problem to the student. You see, even if they lived a long time, nevertheless from the time they heard the words, "Earth thou art, and to earth thou shalt return" and received the sentence of death, they became liable to death and you would say from that moment they were dead.

Ib., (41, 42). pp. 243-244.

[72] "Adam called the name of his wife Life, [Eve, ζωὴ] because she was the mother of all living." See the precision of Sacred Scripture, how it did not pass over even this detail, but taught us that Adam named his wife as well ...She is the source of all those who will come from her, the root and foundation of the future race. Then, after teaching us the naming of the woman, it further shows us God's goodness, how He does not overlook them in their depth of shame and nakedness after being created by Him. "The Lord made for Adam and his wife garments of skin," the text says, "and clothed them" ...The loving God ...showed them great pity and had mercy on their fall: seeing them covered in confusion and ignorant of what to do to avoid being naked and feeling ashamed, He makes garments of skin for them and clothes them in them ...

[73] Let us understand "made" in the sense of 'gave directions for': He ordered that they be clad in garments of skin as a constant reminder of their disobedience. Let the affluent pay heed, those who pamper themselves with cloth from the silkworm and are clad in silk, and let them learn how at the beginning from the outset the loving Lord instructed the human race: when the first-formed man became liable to punishment of death

through the Fall and the Lord had to clothe him in a garment to hide his shame, he made them garments of skin, to teach us to shun the soft and dissolute life, and not to pine for one that is lazy and characterized by inactivity, but rather strive for an austere life.

Homily 18 on Genesis (3, 4, 5), CUA Vol. 82, pp. 4-6.

[74] "Behold, Adam is become as one of us." Great is the reproach in this sentence, capable of touching the heart of the transgressor. Was this your reason, He is saying, for despising My command, that you had notions of equality? Lo, you have become what you expected - or rather not what you expected but what you deserved to become ...This, in fact, is what the guileful devil said to them through the serpent, that "Your eyes would be opened, and ye would be as gods, knowing good and evil."

[75] "Now lest at any time he stretch forth his hand, and take of the tree of life and eat, and so he shall live for ever." See here, I ask you, the Lord's loving kindness. I mean, we must study the saying precisely so that nothing concealed under the surface can escape us. When God gave Adam the command, He bade him abstain from nothing, with the single exception of that tree, and when he presumed to taste it he received the sentence of death; He made this clear to him in giving him the command in case he should break it, though He had given him no express instruction about the tree of life. I mean, since He created him immortal, as I see it and you can understand, it would have been possible for Adam, if he had wanted, to partake of that tree along with the others, a tree that was able to provide him with endless life - hence he was given no instruction about it.

[76] If, however, someone of a meddling nature should inquire why it was called the tree of life, let him learn that it was not possible for human beings to discern all God's works precisely by following their own reasoning. The Lord, you see, decided that the human being created by Him should have some practice in disobedience and obedience while living in the garden, and decided to provide examples there of these two trees, one of life, the other of death (so to say) in the sense that tasting it and breaking the command brought death on him. So when by partaking of this tree he became liable to death and subject in the future to the needs of the body, and the entry of sin had its beginnings as the result of which death also was fittingly provided for by the Lord, no longer did He allow Adam in the garden but bade him leave there, showing us that His sole motive in doing this was His love for him ...

[77] Since [Adam] had given signs of considerable intemperance through the command already given him (He is saying) and had become subject to death, lest he presume further to lay hold of this tree which offers endless life and go on sinning forever, it would be better for him to be driven from here. And so the expulsion from the garden was a mark of care

rather than necessity ...To check our decline into greater evil and to stem the tide of wickedness, He applies punishment out of fidelity to His own lovingkindness.
Ib., (6, 7, 8, 9), pp. 7-8.

7. St. Athanasius of Alexandria:
[78] When Adam had transgressed, his sin reached unto all men.
Four Discourses Against the Arians, I, 51, NPNF Vol. IV SS p. 336.

8. St. Irenaeus of Lyons:
[79] How is it possible to say that the serpent, created by God dumb and irrational, was endowed with reason and speech? For if it had the power of itself to speak, to discern, to understand, and to reply to what was spoken by the woman, there would have been nothing to prevent every serpent from doing this also. If, however, they say again that it was according to the divine will and dispensation that this serpent spoke with a human voice to Eve, they render God the author of sin. Neither was it possible for the evil demon to impart speech to a speechless nature, and thus from that which is not to produce that which is; for if that were the case, he never would have ceased (with the view of leading man astray) from conferring with and deceiving them by means of serpents, and beasts, and birds.

[80] From what quarter, too, did it, being a beast, obtain information regarding the injunction of God to the man given to him alone, and in secret, not even the woman herself being aware of it?*

Why also did it not prefer to make its attack upon the man instead of the woman? And if you say that it attacked her as being the weaker of the two, on the contrary, she was the stronger, since she appears to have been the helper of the man in the transgression of the commandment. For she did by herself alone resist the serpent, and it was after holding out for a while and making opposition that she ate of the tree, being circumvented by craft; whereas Adam, making no fight whatever, nor refusal, partook of the fruit handed to him by the woman ...

And the woman indeed, having been vanquished in the contest by a demon, is deserving of pardon; but Adam should deserve none, for he was worsted by the woman - he who, in his own person, had received the command from God.

But the woman, having heard of the command from Adam, treated it with contempt, either because she deemed it unworthy of God to speak by means of it, or because she had her doubts, perhaps even held the opinion

---

*St. Irenaeus is probably referring to the chronology in Genesis 2:16 and 2:22, which would indicate that the injunction about the tree was given to Adam before Eve was created. Also see 3:18.

that the command was given to her by Adam of his own accord. The serpent found her working alone, so that it was enabled to confer with her apart. Observing her then either eating or not eating from the trees, he put before her the fruit of the [forbidden] tree.

[81] And if it saw her eating, it is manifest that she was partaker of a body subject to corruption. "For everything going into the mouth is cast out into the draught" (Mt. 15:17). If then corruptible, it is obvious that she was also mortal. But if mortal, then there was certainly no curse, nor was that a [condemnatory] sentence, when the voice of God spoke to the man, "For earth thou art and to earth thou shalt return," as the true course of things proceeds [now and always].

Then again, if the serpent observed the woman not eating, how did he induce her to eat who never had eaten? And who pointed out to this accursed man-slaying serpent that the sentence of death pronounced against them by God would not take [immediate] effect, when He said, "For the day that ye eat thereof, ye shall surely die"? And not merely this, but that along with the impunity the eyes of those should be opened who had not seen until then? But with the opening [of their eyes] referred to, they made entrance upon the path of death.

Fragments of the Lost Writings of Irenaeus (XVI). ANF, Vol. 1, pp. 570-571.

[82] The Lord then was manifestly coming to His own things, and was sustaining them by means of that creation which is supported by Himself, and was making a recapitulation of that disobedience which had occurred in connection with a tree, through the obedience which was [exhibited by Himself when He hung] upon a tree. [The effects] also of that deception being done away with, by which that virgin Eve, who was already espoused to a man, was unhappily misled - was happily announced, through means of the truth by the angel to the Virgin Mary, who was [also espoused] to a man. For just as the former was led astray by the word of an angel, so that she fled from God when she had transgressed His word, so did the latter, by an angelic communication, receive the glad tidings that she should sustain God, being obedient to His word. And if the former did disobey God, yet the latter was persuaded to be obedient to God, in order that the Virgin Mary might become the patroness of the virgin Eve. And so, as the human race fell into bondage to death by means of a virgin, so it is rescued by a virgin; virginal disobedience having been balanced in the opposite scale by virginal obedience. For in the same way the sin of the first created man receives amendment by the correction of the First-begotten, and the coming of the serpent is conquered by the harmlessness of the dove, those bonds being unloosed by which we had been fast bound by death.

Against Heresies, Book V, Chapter XIX (1), Ibid., p. 547.

[83]Those, therefore, who desert the preaching of the Church, call in question the knowledge of the holy presbyters, not taking into consideration of how much greater consequence is a religious man, even in a private station, than a blasphemous and impudent sophist. Now, such are all the heretics and those who imagine that they have hit upon something more beyond the truth ...

It behoves us, therefore, to avoid their doctrines, and to take careful heed lest we suffer any injury from them, but to flee to the Church, and be brought up in her bosom, and be nourished with the Lord's Scriptures. For the Church has been planted as a garden (*paradisus*) in this world. Therefore says the Spirit of God, "Thou mayest freely eat from every tree of the garden," that is, Eat from every Scripture of the Lord, but you shall not eat with an uplifted mind, nor touch any heretical discord. For these men do profess that they have themselves the knowledge of good and evil, and they set their own impious minds above the God who made them. They therefore form opinions on what is beyond the limits of the understanding. For this cause also the apostle says, "Be not wise beyond what it is fitting to be wise, but be wise prudently," (cf. Rom. 12:3), so that we be not cast forth by eating of the "knowledge" of these men (that knowledge which knows more than it should do) from the paradise of life.

Into this paradise, the Lord has introduced those who obey His call, "summing up in Himself all things which are in heaven, and which are on earth" (cf. Eph. 1:10), but the things in heaven are spiritual, while those on earth constitute the dispensation in human nature. These things, therefore, He recapitulated in Himself: by uniting man to the Spirit, and causing the Spirit to dwell in man.

Ibid., Chapter XX (2), p. 548.

9. Bishop Nikolai Velimirovich:

[84] The more seriously you war against Him, the more unimpededly is He drawn out of you. The Lord withdraws His strength out of you, as well as His beauty, His health, His wisdom and His blessedness. This is the way the Most High Lord wars with His adversaries.

What remains of you, embattled battlers, once the Lord has drawn out from you what is His? Does anything remain other than weakness, ugliness, sickness, madness, and wretchedness? The Lord will not take from you anything of what is yours. And what is yours is weakness. And once He takes away His power, which you are abusing, He will leave you with your own sepulchral weakness, which can be neither used nor abused.

The Lord will pull His health out of you, and your blood will be transformed into sweat, and your odor will be pleasing to worms, an odor that will cause cities to close their gates ...

Like a child, He is powerless to do evil. He does not return evil for evil, for He is destitute when it comes to evil. Instead He merely gathers His good gifts and walks off with them.

Prayers by the Lake, LXXXII, The Treasury of Serbian Orthodox Spirituality, translated by Rt. Rev. Todor Mika and V. Rev. Dr. Stevan Scott, Vol. V, pp. 158-160.

10. St. Ambrose of Milan:

[85] God cast Adam out of Paradise immediately after his fault; there was no delay. At once the fallen were severed from all their enjoyment, that they might do penance; at once God clothed them with garments of skins, not of silk.

And what reason is there for putting off? Is it that you may sin yet more? Then because God is good you are evil, and "despise the riches of His goodness and long-suffering" (Rom. 2:4). But the goodness of the Lord ought rather to draw you to repentance. For this reason holy David says to all: "Come, let us worship and fall down before Him, and mourn before our Lord who made us" (cf. Ps. 94 [95]:6) ...

But nothing causes such exceeding grief as when anyone, lying under the captivity of sin, calls to mind from where he has fallen, because he turned aside to carnal and earthly things, instead of directing his mind in the beautiful ways of the knowledge of God. So you find Adam concealing himself, when he knew that God was present and wishing to be hidden when called by God with that voice which wounded the soul of him who was hiding: "Adam, where art thou?" That is to say, Why do you hide yourself? Why are you concealed? Why do you avoid Him Whom you once longed to see? A guilty conscience is so burdensome that it punishes itself without a judge, and wishes for covering, and yet is bare before God.

Concerning Repentance, Book II, Chap. XI (99-103), NPNF, Vol. X SS, p. 357-358.

GENESIS, CHAPTER 4, Selected Verses (Septuagint)

[86] *4:1: And Adam knew Eve his wife, and she conceived and brought forth Cain and said, I have gained a man through God.* [1]

4:2: And she again bore his brother Abel. And Abel was a keeper of sheep, but Cain was a tiller of the ground ... [1, 2]

4:3 And it was so after some time that Cain brought of the fruits of the earth a sacrifice to the Lord. [1, 2]

4:4 And Abel also brought of the firstborn of his sheep and of his fatlings, and God looked upon Abel and his gifts,

4:5 but Cain and his sacrifices he regarded not, and Cain was exceedingly sorrowful and his countenance fell.

4:6 And the Lord God said to Cain, Why art thou become very sorrowful and why is thy countenance fallen?

4:7 Hast thou not sinned if thou hast brought it rightly, but not rightly divided it? be still, to thee shall be his submission, and thou shalt rule over him.

4:8 And Cain said to Abel his brother, Let us go out into the plain; and it came to pass that when they were in the plain Cain rose up against Abel his brother, and slew him.

4:9 And the Lord God said to Cain, Where is Abel thy brother? and he said, I know not, am I my brother's keeper?

4:10 And the Lord said, What hast thou done? the voice of thy brother's blood cries to me out of the ground.

4:11 And now thou art cursed from the earth which has opened her mouth to receive thy brother's blood from thy hand ...

4:12 When thou tillest the earth, then it shall not continue to give its strength to thee: thou shalt be groaning and trembling on the earth.

4:13 And Cain said to the Lord God, My crime is too great for me to be forgiven.

4:14 If Thou castest me out this day from the face of the earth, and I shall be hidden from Thy presence, and I shall be groaning and trembling upon the earth, then it will be that any one that finds me shall slay me.

4:15 And the Lord God said to him, Not so, any one that slays Cain shall suffer seven-fold vengeance; and the Lord God set a mark upon Cain, that no one that found him might slay him.

4:16 So Cain went forth from the presence of God and dwelt in the land of Nod over against Edem. [2]

4:17 And Cain knew his wife, and having conceived she bore Enoch ...

4:18 And to Enoch was born Gaidad; and Gaidad begot Maleleel; and Maleleel begot Mathusala; and Mathusala begot Lamech ...

4:23: And Lamech said to his wives, Ada and Sella, Hear my voice, ye wives of Lamech, consider my words, because I have slain a man to my sorrow and a youth to my grief.

4:24: Because vengeance has been exacted seven times on Cain's behalf, on Lamech's it shall be seventy times seven.

4:25: And Adam knew Eve his wife, and she conceived and bore a son, and called his name Seth, saying, For God has raised up to me another seed instead of Abel, whom Cain slew. [1, 2]

4:26: And Seth had a son, and he called his name Enos: he hoped to call on the name of the Lord God. [1, 2, 3]

The Fathers on Genesis 4

1. St. John Chrysostom:
[87] I will ensure, He is saying, that the generation of children, a reason for great satisfaction, for you will begin with pain, so that each time without fail you will personally have a reminder, through the distress and the pain of each birth, of the magnitude of this sin of disobedience, and may not in the course of time allow the event to slip into oblivion, but may be enabled to realize that the deception was the cause of these ills.
Homily 17 on Genesis (31), CUA, Vol. 74, p. 238.

[88] "And Adam knew Eve his wife." Consider when this happened. After their disobedience, after their loss of the garden, then it was that the practice of intercourse had its beginning. You see, before their disobedience they followed a life like that of the angels, and there was no mention of intercourse. How could there be, when they were not subject to the needs of the body? So, at the outset and from the beginning the practice of virginity was in force; but when through their indifference disobedience came on the scene and the ways of sin were opened, virginity took its leave for the reason that they had proved unworthy of such a degree of good things, and in its place the practice of intercourse took over for the future ...Do you see how those who have followed the vocation to virginity for the love of Christ imitate the life of angels through treading the earth and being clad in a body? I mean, the greater and more elevated the task, so much and even greater the laurels, the rewards and the good things promised to those who give evidence of the practice of good works along with this vocation.
Homily 18 on Genesis (12), CUA Vol. 82, pp. 10, 11.

[89] She said, "I have gained a man through God." See how the imposition of the punishment brought the woman to her senses? She attributes

the child she bore not to a natural process but to God, and displays her own gratitude. Do you see how the punishment proved an occasion of admonition to them? ...It was not nature, she is saying, that presented me with the child, instead, grace from above has given him to me.

[90] "And she again bore his brother Abel." Since she proved to be grateful for the birth of the first child and acknowledged the former kindness, she enjoyed the good fortune of a second. Our Lord is like this, you see: when we display gratitude for previous good deeds and acknowledge the benefactor, He lavishes His gifts upon us more generously. Accordingly, because she attributed the birth to God, for that reason she receives another child. You see, the generation of children was the greatest consolation from then on, once mortality had come on the scene. For this reason, of course, the loving God at once and from the beginning reduced the severity of their punishment and stripped away the fearsome visage of death by favoring them with the propagation of children, foreshadowing, as it were, in this event an image of resurrection and ensuring that others would rise up in place of the fallen.

Ibid. (12, 14, 15), pp. 11-12.

[91] The text says, "Cain brought of the fruits of the earth a sacrifice to the Lord." He knew and understood that he should offer from his own possessions some produce to God as to his master, not because God needs them, but for the purpose of demonstrating his gratitude as being himself a beneficiary of such kindness ...

[92] Let us attend with precision, dearly beloved, to the text and see what Scripture says about Cain on the one hand and Abel on the other, and let us not pass it by heedlessly. I mean Sacred Scripture says nothing idly or by chance; instead, even if it happens to be a syllable or a single jot, it has some treasure concealed in it. Such, after all, is the nature of all things spiritual ...

Wanting to teach us about Abel as well, Sacred Scripture says that he for his part also brought his offering from his occupation and his shepherding. "And Abel also brought of the firstborn of his sheep and of his fatlings." Notice how it hints to us of the piety of this man's attitude, and the fact that he did not casually offer any one of his sheep, but "of the firstborn," that is, from the valuable and special ones. In Cain's case, on the contrary, nothing of the kind is suggested; rather, the fact that he "brought of the fruits of the earth," as if to say, whatever came to hand, without any display of zeal or precise care ...

[93] The person who through indifference betrayed his own welfare duly pays the penalty. I mean, it was not a case of one man having a teacher and the other having a counsellor and adviser: each had instructions from his own conscience, and being moved by the intelligence supplied to the

human race from above he proceeded to make his offering, such as it was; but the difference in attitude that emerged and the medium of choice caused one man's offering to be acceptable and the other's to be spurned ...

[94] See how in this case is fulfilled the saying in the gospel that the first will be last and the last first (cf. Mk 10:32; Mt. 19:30, Lk. 13:30). I mean, see how the one who enjoyed priority belonging to the firstborn and consequently made his offering first was shown to be inferior to his brother since he made it unworthily: as both presented their offerings, Sacred Scripture says, "God looked upon Abel and his gifts." What does that mean, "looked upon"? He accepted, He approved of the attitude, He rewarded the choice, He was satisfied (so to say) with what was done. You see, we speak about God and presume to open our mouth about that pure nature, yet being human we would have no choice but to understand these things through language ...God took notice of him for the reason that he had made the offering with a pure intention, and of his gifts for the reason not only that they were free of imperfection but that they were in every respect clearly precious, both from the viewpoint of the offeror's intention and from the fact of their being the firstborn and in fact specially selected from them, among the fattest of them and the very prize ones ...

[95] Notice the precision of Sacred Scripture: by the phrase "He regarded not" it shows us the rejection of what was offered, and by calling what was offered from the soil a sacrifice he teaches us something else again. I mean, see how He shows us through the very events and terms that the Lord wants all these things to be done by us so that the kind of intention we have should be made clear through the actions we take, and so that we may be in a position to know that we are subject to a Lord and Creator who brought us from nothing to being.

Ib., (14, 15, 16, 17, 18, 19, 20), pp. 11-15.

[96] "She conceived and bore a son," the text says, "and called his name Seth". The mother was not content with giving the name but added, "For God has raised up to me another seed instead of Abel, whom Cain slew." Notice also the mother, how through the name of the child she bore she ensures a constant reminder of that evil deed, and, so that future generations may be in a position to know of the crime committed by Cain, she says, "in place of Abel, whom Cain slew." The comment of a grieving spirit, upset at the memory of what had happened, and while thankful for her new child, yet by the name she gave it erecting a monument, as it were, to her other son. After all, it was no chance sorrow he brought to his parents in raising his hand against his brother and stretching him on the ground before their eyes, a lifeless corpse, whom they had bred and cherished. I mean, if Adam received the sentence, "earth thou art and to earth thou shalt return," and "in whatever day ye eat of it, ye shall surely die," still the meaning of the sen-

tence lay in the words alone for the time being and he had no awareness up
to that point of what death looked like. Cain, on the contrary, took the initiative against his brother out of hatred, let loose against Abel the rancor
that had been gnawing at his vitals, and thus provided his parents with a
dreadful spectacle to contemplate. For this reason, assuredly, the mother,
who had scarcely lifted her head and was able only at this late stage to find
some consolation for that unbearable grief in the birth of a son, offered
thanks to the Lord and immortalized the crime of fratricide, thus also in-
flicting on him the severest of punishments by ensuring the unfailing
remembrance of what had been done by him ...

[97] "And Seth had a son," the text goes on; "and he called his name
Enos [Enosh]: he hoped to call on the name of the Lord God." See how
people are now taught to incorporate an expression of their own gratitude
in the names of their children ...You see, from this person onwards the
blessed author is on the point of beginning the genealogy, having dismissed
the memory of Cain and also of those who were descended from him up to
Lamech; since he had by the evil of his course of action besmirched the
prerogative granted to him by nature - I mean that of firstborn - he is ex-
punged from the list along with his descendants. Now Seth, on the contrary, is accorded this distinction - something he did not enjoy by nature -
on account of gratitude in his course of action, and for the future the position of firstborn is transferred to him, if not by nature, at least by the attitude revealed in his course of action, and those descended from him are
accorded a place in the genealogy. Just as the son is called Enos [Enosh]
through invoking the name of the Lord God, so too those who continue the
line from him in future are accorded the same name. Hence this blessed
author concludes the narrative at this stage and then begins another.

Homily 20 on Genesis (13, 15), Ibid., pp. 44-46.

2. St. Didymus the Blind:

[98] The soul, when it falls into error and sin, engenders evil progeny
(Cain), but if the mind, returned to sobriety, effects a conversion, then quite
evidently, the soul begins by rejecting that offspring and by conceiving the
entrance into virtue (Abel), which indeed is praiseworthy. Then, growing
little by little through progress, it will arrive one day at perfection; but it is
detestable, inversely, after virtue has begun, to add evil by a perversion of
noble thought.

Happily, too, the Scripture has recorded their mode of life. "Abel was
a keeper of sheep, but Cain was a tiller of the ground." This statement
evokes, in the historical sense, a remark that is not negligible if we observe
the order in which the two brothers are named. For in regard to birth, Cain
is first, in accord with the requirements of chronology, but in regard to oc-
cupations the just one has the leading place. For the occupation of Abel

was noble and more honorable than that of Cain, because living beings surpass inanimate ones in the principles of natural diversity...

Cain is not said to be a farmer, but a laborer of the ground, for he was not noble as was Noah, who is called a farmer and not a laborer (cf. Gen. 9:20).

According to allegory, Abel is a shepherd of animals, that is of the senses, leading them by knowledge as an excellent shepherd, and imposing reason on the irascible and concupiscible like a conductor or a director. Cain, who moved about on the ground and in earthly matters, is not called a cultivator - for even concerning these things he did not seek order. But it states "tiller of the ground" and nothing more, because he was a lover of the body, possessing neither reason nor order...

Because Cain had made his offering negligently, and Abel in a sincere manner "God looked upon Abel and his gifts, but Cain and his sacrifices He regarded not." For Abel's sincerity is manifest: he offers of his firstborn, considering it necessary to reserve for God the most precious things, from which he also chose the fatlings. This is what Cain should have done, bringing the firstfruits of the fields. For it is especially appropriate to offer the firstfruits to God ...

That, therefore, is the literal explanation. The anagogic sense would be as follows. Those who simulate virtue in exhibiting a pleasing exterior, without a sincere motive, but for the sake of something else, are temporizers and are fraudulant, because they fail to offer their firstfruits to God. The firstfruits of virtue are those which come from intention, for the movement towards virtue grows from this. David teaches this in saying: "His desire is in the law of the Lord" (cf. Ps. 1:2), while the hypocrites who do not have the desire for virtue simulate virtuous things for shameful gain, as it is written, or for [empty] glory. Cain, who belongs to this category, offered "after some time"; Abel, on the contrary, offered without delay firstborn animals and fatlings, because the virtuous man, in the firstfruits of his actions, deems that there is nothing that is not to be referred to God, as the blessed Paul also thinks when he says: "It was not through me, but the grace of God in me" (cf. Eph. 3:7-8, 1 Cor. 15:10), and the Psalmist: "Except the Lord build the house, they labor in vain that build it" (Ps. 126 [127]:1).

Sur la Genèse, VIII, 7, 8, 9, 10, pp. 279-287.

[99] We do not understand that Cain "went forth from the presence of God" in a local sense, but we say that every sinner puts himself outside of God. Thus also we understand the expression "to enter in" toward God, when the Psalmist says "Let us come before His presence with thanksgiving" (Ps. 94 [95]:2); one "comes before the presence" of God... leaving all things that are outside of Him, sin and sense-perceptible things, to become other than the world, and thus to participate in the knowledge of that which is of

God. So then it reads: "Cain went forth from the presence of God", and we do not claim that there is a certain place where God is, where Cain was, and from where he departed; for God is not circumscribable nor confined to space, although a temple was later made [to Him], which was a school teaching symbolic adoration.

Cain went forth, therefore, having rendered himself unworthy of the presence of God: that is, there was no longer for him any spiritual ascent. Concerning such persons, it is written "God is not before them" ...

We recall that when discussing Adam's expulsion from Paradise, we remarked that God drove him out, because he had not departed on his own, but he still had a spark of desire to live in the Paradise of delight. This is why God let him live in His sight as he himself managed his household; for to those who do not have major sins, virtue is not far away, and God gives the occasion and the suggestion to make a speedy return to Himself. However, this is not said of Cain: God neither let him dwell nearby, nor drove him away, but by a voluntary desire he slipped away toward evil..

Ibid., IX, 7, 8, pp. 313-315.

[100] It often happens that saints born of a saint retain from him birth both according to the flesh and according to the soul. In this way Abraham became the father of Isaac, Isaac of Jacob, and Jacob of Joseph; for they are descended from them in a human sense and also imitators of their virtue. Esau was begotten of Isaac only according to the flesh, since he was a stranger to him in intentions, for he became worthless. Seth, then, born to replace a just man, generates Enos: the just engendering one who is just; and the latter, instead of having a proper name of his own, is called 'man.' Such a naming demonstrates the virtue of his soul which preserved that which was "in the image," and the truly real state of man, for in Hebrew Enos signifies 'man.'

Indeed the Scripture also attributes to him that which is characteristic of man: "he hoped to call on* ($\H{\eta}\lambda\pi\iota\sigma\epsilon\nu$ $\epsilon\pi\iota\kappa\alpha\lambda\epsilon\tilde{\iota}\sigma\theta\alpha\iota$) the name of the Lord." Now that is activity appropriate to a virtuous man. True hope is to desire to be as much like God as possible, and to hope to call on the name of the Lord also indicates one who subjects himself to the divine authority and teaching...

One should not be surprised that Enos and Adam both signify 'man,' for in Hebrew the man has several names, just as those who speak Greek

---

* Note: related to $\epsilon\pi\iota\kappa\alpha\lambda\epsilon\omega$ is also the word epiclesis [$\epsilon\pi\iota\kappa\lambda\eta\sigma\iota\varsigma$]: the central part of the Orthodox liturgy, in which the priest calls upon the Holy Spirit to change the bread and the wine into the body and blood of Christ. As the late Father Alexander Schmemann pointed out in "For the Life of the World" in commenting on the call of the priest "Thine of Thine own we offer unto Thee," man is a priest. He stands in the center of the world and unifies it in his act of blessing God, of both receiving the world from God and offering it to God.

call him *anthropos, merops, brotos, phota*: all these words, which correspond to etymologies, are natural names and not merely conventional names...

The Psalmist says: "The days of our years are three score years and ten; and if by reason of strength they be four score years, yet is their strength labor and sorrow" (Ps. 89 [90]:10). For after eighty years, life is pain and weariness. But then they did not age quickly: at a hundred and sixty years one appeared to be in the prime of life. And probably in the beginning men attained long lives, lest if they died prematurely the human race could have failed, since it stemmed from a single source. For thus they produced more children, since the duration of their life was longer, but Scripture only mentions one [descendant] among others because, in the matter of succession, one names only the firstborn. If it is objected that Seth was the third and not the firstborn, it is necessary to respond that it was not fitting to begin with Cain, who was worthless, nor with Abel who died without progeny, but with Seth who was also in a certain manner the firstborn.

Sur la Genèse, Vol. I, IX, 16, X, 1, pp. 331-333; Vol. II, X, 2, 3, pp. 11-13.

3. Bishop Nikolai Velimirovich:

[101] "And Mary said: 'Behold the handmaid of the Lord'" (Lk. 1:38).

Here indeed, my brethren, is the handmaid of the Lord! If a handmaid is one who submits her will utterly to that of her Lord, then the most Holy Virgin is first among the Lord's handmaids. If a handmaid is one who strives with all her heart to serve her Lord, then, again, she is first among the Lord's handmaids. If a handmaid is one who meekly and silently endures all insults and trials, looking only to the reward from her Lord, then, again and again, the Holy Virgin is the first and most excellent of all the Lord's handmaids. She was not concerned to please the world but to please God; not to stand well in the world's eyes, but only in God's. She was the epitome of obedience, service and meekness. The most holy Virgin could with truth say to the angel: "Behold the handmaid of the Lord." The greatest perfection and the greatest honor to which a woman can attain on earth is to be a handmaid of the Lord. Eve lost this perfection and honor in Paradise without effort, and the Virgin Mary achieved this perfection and honor outside Paradise by her efforts.

At the prayers of the holy Virgin and Mother of God, O Lord Jesus, have mercy on us. To Thee be glory and praise for ever. Amen.

The Prologue from Ochrid, December 26th, Vol. 4, pp. 374-375.

GENESIS, CHAPTER 5, (Septuagint)

[102] *5:1: This is the genealogy of men in the day in which God made Adam; in the image of God He made him:* [1]

5:2: male and female He made them, and blessed them; and He called his name Adam, in the day in which He made them.

5:3: And Adam lived two hundred and thirty years, and begot a son after his own form, and after his own image, and he called his name Seth. [1]

5:4: And the days of Adam, which he lived after his begetting of Seth, were seven hundred years; and he begot sons and daughters.

5:5: And all the days of Adam which he lived were nine hundred and thirty years, and he died.

5:6: Now Seth lived two hundred and five years, and begot Enos.

5:7: And Seth lived after his begetting Enos, seven hundred and seven years, and he begot sons and daughters.

5:8: And all the days of Seth were nine hundred and twelve years, and he died.

5:9: And Enos lived an hundred and ninety years, and begot Cainan.

5:10: And Enos lived after his begetting Cainan, seven hundred amd fifteen years, and he begot sons and daughters.

5:11: And all the days of Enos were nine hundred and five years, and he died.

5:12: And Cainan lived an hundred and seventy years, and he begot Maleleel.

5:13: And Cainan lived after his begetting Maleleel, seven hundred and forty years, and he begot sons and daughters.

5:14: And all the days of Cainan were nine hundred and ten years, and he died.

5:15: And Maleleel lived an hundred and sixty and five years, and he begot Jared.

5:16: And Maleleel lived after his begetting Jared, seven hundred and thirty years, and he begot sons and daughters.

5:17: And all the days of Maleleel were eight hundred and ninety and five years, and he died.

5:18: And Jared lived an hundred and sixty and two years, and begot Enoch:

5:19: And Jared lived after his begetting Enoch, eight hundred years, and he begot sons and daughters.

5:20: And all the days of Jared were nine hundred and sixty and two years, and he died.

5:21: And Enoch lived an hundred and sixty and five years and begat Mathusala.

5:22: And Enoch was well-pleasing to God after his begetting Mathusala, two hundred years, and he begot sons and daughters.

5:23: And all the days of Enoch were three hundred and sixty and five years.

5:24: And Enoch was well-pleasing to God, and was not found, because God translated him. [1, 2]

5:25: And Mathusala lived an hundred and sixty and seven years, and begot Lamech.

5:26: And Mathusala lived after his begetting Lamech eight hundred and two years, and begot sons and daughters.

5:27: And all the days of Mathusala which he lived, were nine hundred and sixty and nine years, and he died.

5:28: And Lamech lived an hundred and eighty and eight years, and begot a son.

5:29: And he called his name Noe [Noah], saying, This one will cause us to cease from our works, and from the toils of our hands, and from the earth, which the Lord God has cursed. [1]

5:30: And Lamech lived after his begetting Noe, five hundred and sixty and five years, and begot sons and daughters.

5:31: And all the days of Lamech were seven hundred and fifty three years and he died.

6:1: And Noe was five hundred years old, and he begot three sons, Sem, Cham, and Japheth.

The Fathers on Genesis 5

1. St. John Chrysostom:

[103] Wonderful and beyond telling, dearly beloved, is the treasure in the words read just now. I realize that for their part many people take one look at a list of names, pay attention only to the surface of the text, and judge that the words contain nothing more than simply a list of names ...I guarantee to show you a wealth of thought hidden there. You see, there is not even a syllable or even one letter contained in Scripture which does not have great treasure concealed in its depths. Hence we must be guided by grace from above and accept the enlightenment of the Holy Spirit, and only then approach the divine sayings ...

[104] Notice how he employs the same words as in the beginning to teach us that he did not even rate worth a mention from now on those generations turned reprobate; instead, he begins the genealogy from the later-born child - I mean Seth - so that from this fact also you may learn how much store God sets by human nature and how he abhors people of murderous intent. You see, he passes over mention of them as if they were people never brought into existence, thus showing us how terrible wicked-

44

ness is and the fact that those who embrace it do the worst harm to themselves ...

[105] He wanted to console Adam, so to say, for finding himself so desolated not only by his own fall but also by Cain's crime which he saw with his own eyes. Not that they knew what death looked like, even if they had received the sentence: a twofold and threefold grief afflicted him because he saw death introduced into life for the first time, violent death at that, perpetrated by his own son, against his brother, of the same mother and same father as himself, one who had done him no ill. Accordingly, the loving God, wishing to bring him some consolation to compensate him for those griefs, provided him with another son, Seth, and in supplying adequate solace for him by that means he guarantees for the future the beginning of another line from him. Hence the blessed author made that opening remark, "This is the genealogy of men."
Homily 18 on Genesis (1, 4, 6). CUA Vol. 82, pp. 50, 51, 53, 54, 55.

Adam "begot a son after his own form, and after his own image," he says, "and he called his name Seth." In the case of the previous child - I mean Cain - on the contrary, he made no such comment except to suggest at the beginning his decline into evil ...It is not in reference to bodily features that Scripture is speaking to us here in the words, "a son ...after his own image;" it is to do with the disposition of his soul, so that we may learn that he would not turn out like the other brother.

[106] For this reason, too, his mother in giving her son this name did so with thanks, attributing the birth of a son not to nature or to the process of birth but to the power of God ...See the precision of the expression; she did not say, God has given me, but "God has raised up to me." Notice how in outline a premonition of the resurrection is already being suggested to us through this expression. I mean, she spoke as if to say, He has raised up this child for me in place of the fallen one ...

[107] Let women not be distressed when they have no children; instead, let them give evidence of the thankful disposition and have recourse to the Creator and direct their request to him, the Lord of nature, not attributing childbirth to the intercourse of the partners, nor any other source than the Creator of everything, who also brings our nature from non-being into being and is able to correct anything deficient. This is exemplified in Eve's making the fact of her grief an occasion for praise when she attributes everything to the Lord ...

[108] He not only favors her with another son but also predicts at this point that he will be virtuous. He "begot a son," the text says, remember, "...after his own image." For an immediate insight into the child's virtue, notice him also in turn demonstrating the piety of his attitude in the name of his child. "Seth had a son, and he called his name Enos [Enosh]: he

hoped to call on the name of the Lord" ...What in fact could be more blessed than this man adorned by God himself with this title and employing it in place of a name?

[109] Do you see how ...in these mere names a great wealth of thought lies hidden? That is to say, they reveal in this case not simply the piety of the parents but also the great concern they had for their children, and how from the very beginning they instructed the children born to them through the names they gave them to cling to virtue. They did not give names casually and by chance, like people today ...The ancients, on the contrary, did not act that way; instead, they took great pains to give such names to their children as not merely led to virtue in those receiving them but proved instructive in complete wisdom for everybody else and for later generations also.

Ibid., (7, 8, 9, 10), pp. 55, 56, 57.

[110] Enoch pleased God, and he was "not found because God translated him." Was I not right in saying that as we proceeded we would find immense spiritual riches beyond all telling in these names? Consider at this point, I ask you, dearly beloved, the just man's virtue, the good God's love exceeding all limits, and the precision of Sacred Scripture. "Enoch lived an hundred and sixty and five years," the text says, "and begat Mathusala. And Enoch was well-pleasing to God after his begetting Mathusala."

[111] Let both men and women listen and learn about the just man's virtue, and not consider marriage to be an obstacle to pleasing God. I mean, it was to this effect that in more than one place Sacred Scripture made a point of saying that he had a son Mathusala and then pleased God, and said the same thing over again in the words, "was well-pleasing to God after his begetting Mathusala," in case anyone thought it was an obstacle to virtue. You see, as long as we are on our guard, neither marriage nor bringing up children nor anything else will be able to stand in the way of our being pleasing to God ...Dearly beloved, had marriage or the raising of children been likely to prove a stumbling block on the way to virtue, the Creator of all would not have introduced marriage into our life lest it prove our undoing in difficult times and through severe problems. Since, however, family life not only offers us no obstacle to wisdom in God's eyes as long as we are prepared to be on our guard, but even brings us much encouragement and calms the tumult of our natural tendencies, not allowing the billows to surge but constantly ensuring that the barque dock safely in the harbor, consequently he granted the human race the consolation that comes from this source ...

[112] Since, after the fall of the first-formed, a human being was found to ascend the very heights of virtue and to revoke the sin of our first parents through his own acceptable way of life, see the exceeding love of the good

God. When He found someone capable of revoking Adam's sin, He showed through his very actions that it was not out of a desire to inflict death on our race for transgression of the command that He had condemned the person who had been given the command; He took him away during his lifetime to another place. "Enoch was well-pleasing to God," the text says, "and was not found, because God translated him." Do you see the Lord's wisdom? He took him away during his lifetime. He did not grant him immortality, in case this should diminish fear of sinning; instead, He let it remain strong in the human race.

[113] Hence once again obscurely, so to say, and imperceptibly He wants the sentence He had passed on Adam to be revoked. But He does not make it obvious, so that fear may have the effect of bringing people to their senses. Consequently, He took away Enoch, who pleased Him. If, however, someone were anxious to be meddlesome and ask, Where did He take him? Has he continued to live till the present? let that person learn not to follow human reasoning or to pry into God's doings but to believe what is said ...God took him during his lifetime without his having experienced death; rather, through the personal satisfaction he found in God's eyes he proved superior to the sentence passed on the race of human beings. But where He took him, or what kind of life he lives now, these further details were not given.

[114] He meant to teach us that, if the other had not paid greater regard to the devil's deceit than to the command given him, he would have been granted the same reward or even greater. "Mathusala lived an hundred and sixty and seven years," the text says, "and begot Lamech." Lamech was a hundred and eighty years old when he had a son; he named him Noe [Noah], saying, "This one will cause us to cease from our works, and from the toils of our hands, and from the earth, which the Lord has cursed." See once again in the name of Lamech's newborn child the greatness of the mysteries, the extraordinary nature of the prophecy, and the good God's unspeakable love. I mean, when by His own prescience He foresees the future, and descries the increase in human beings' wickedness, He foretells by means of the child's name the evils that will come upon all the race of human beings, in the hope that, provided they respond to fear, come to their senses and eschew wickedness, they may choose virtue instead. See also the Lord's longsuffering, how long before the event He makes His prophecy so as to demonstrate His characteristic love and deprive of any excuse those destined to suffer the punishment.

[115] Perhaps, however, someone may say, How did Lamech come to have such a degree of prophetic power? After all, Scripture does not record that he was a person of virtue and remarkable powers, does it? Do not be surprised at that, dearly beloved: the Lord, in His wisdom and inven-

tiveness, frequently permits great and wonderful events to be foretold by unworthy people, not only in the Old Testament but also in the New ...

"And he called his name Noe [Noah]"; his name, you see, means relief, rest. So He is referring to that destruction that was due to occur so many years later as relief - as Job also says, "Death means relief [rest] for man" (cf. Job 3:23 LXX). Since wickedness brings with it great distress of deep intensity, he refers to its removal and disappearance which they were about to experience through that deluge as relief.

Ibid., (11, 12, 13, 14, 15, 16, 17), pp. 58-62.

2. St. Didymus the Blind:

[116] Taking literally the account regarding Enoch, the Apostle says in his Epistle to the Hebrews: "By faith Enoch was translated that he should not see death" (Heb. 11:5). His life was delimited by the same number as the days of a year; then he was translated, which can be understood spiritually by saying that, having acquired perfection and fullness in the virtues required to exist in man, he was translated to a better existence. But this change is not so much made for him but for other men. For these others the body, remaining here below and dissolving, is separated from the soul. Enoch himself, is said to have been translated, and we understand that he was lifted up like Elias [Elijah] or carried off in some other fashion to a divine place.

It is fitting, moreover, to examine here how the words of Paul "It is appointed unto men once to die" (Heb. 9:27) remain true in this case. For if Elias and Enoch were carried away to be now and always in very dense bodies, the words of the wise and holy Paul are untrue according to which all men die. But they are not false. There is a sense which applies to Enoch and Elias, although they did not participate in the death which is now common to other men, one must understand that they are dead in that material life was removed from them in a divine manner that is hidden from us. If the Savior is "firstborn from the dead" (Col. 1:18), He should also be the firstborn of Enoch and Elias, for it would be paradoxical if this principle did not apply to them; besides, if they had not been removed from material life, as we have said, they would not have participated in the divine resurrection, in which we will all receive a body, changed from dishonorable to honorable, from ignoble to glorious, from weak to strong, from earthly (ψυχικοῦ) to spiritual (cf. Phil. 3:21).

Sur la Genèse, Vol. II, X, 4, pp. 15-17. Sources Chrétiennes No. 244.

3. Bishop Nikolai Velimirovich:

"I shall not die, but live, and declare the works of the Lord" (Ps. 117:17). Who can say: "I shall not die"? He who cleaves to the living Lord. Who can positively state: "...But I shall live"? He who sees the living Lord before him. Enoch and Elias did not die, but were caught up into life immortal. The Lord took them in His mercy, and as a proof to men of immortal life. Christ the Lord died and rose again in His might and as a proof to men of resurrection from the dead. The apostles and saints died, but many of them appeared from the other world in their love for men, and as a proof to men of life eternal. Thus both those who were taken up and those who died live with the risen Lord Christ in the immortal Kingdom. "I shall not die, but live," said King David with great certainty, although he lived on earth before the Resurrection of the Lord and the proclamation of the general resurrection of the righteous. Each of us Christians must say with even greater certainty: "I shall not die, but live," because the risen Lord is the foundation of our faith, and because our eyes have seen and our ears have heard more, much more, than the eyes and ears of King David.

The Prologue from Ochrid, October 31, Vol. 4, pp. 135-136.

4. St. Gregory of Nyssa:

[116A] First my mind must become detached from anything subject to flux and change and tranquilly rest in motionless repose, so as to be rendered akin to Him who is perfectly unchangeable; and then it may address Him by this most familiar name and say: Father ...The unjust and impure cannot say Father to the just and pure, since this would mean calling God Father of His own wickedness, which would be nothing but pride ...Hence if a man whose conscience accuses him of evil calls God his Father, he asserts precisely that God is the cause and origin of his own wickedness. But "there is no fellowship of light with darkness," says the Apostle ..."A good tree cannot bring forth evil fruit" (Mt. 7:18) ...If therefore the Lord teaches us in His prayer to call God Father, it seems to me that He is doing nothing else but to set the most sublime life before us as our law. For Truth does not teach us to deceive, to say we are what we are not and to use a name to which we have no right ...Do you see how much preparation we need, and what kind of life we must lead? How ardent must be our zeal so that our conscience may achieve such purity as to have the courage to say "Father" to God? ...How can there be intimacy between the pure and the impure?

The Lord's Prayer. ACW, Vol. #18, pp. 38-40.

THE LAMENT OF EVE

Notes on Genesis, Chapter 5

[117] 1. Relative Ages:

Adam/Eve	Seth	Enos	Cainan	Maleleel	Jared	Enoch	Mathusala
@ 130 yrs	@ 105 yrs	@ 90 yrs	@ 70 yrs	@ 65 yrs	@ 160 yrs	@ 65 yrs	@ 187 yrs

Seth	Enos	Cainan	Maleleel	Jared	Enoch	Mathusala	Lamech
+800	+807	+815	+840	+830	+800	+300	+782
=930	=912	=905	=910	=895	=960	=365	=969

Lamech	Noah
@ 182 yrs	@ 500 yrs
Noah	Shem, Ham, Japheth
+595	Change of life span to 120 years.
777	

Adam/Eve		Age (Accrued):
@ 130 yrs:	Seth	130
+ 105 yrs:	Enos	235
+ 90 yrs:	Cainan	325
+ 70 yrs:	Maleleel	395
+ 65 yrs:	Jared	460
+ 160 yrs:	Enoch	620
+ 65 yrs:	Mathusala	685
+ 187 yrs:	Lamech	872 + 182 yrs: Noah. (Adam = 1054 yrs.i.e.
+ 58 yrs:	Death of Adam	930 Noah was born 124 years after the death of Adam).

Note: The above table is based on the King James Version, i.e., the Hebrew Bible. In the Septuagint, the total years lived for each of the above is the same, but relative ages at the birth of their firstborn are 100 years later. Although the use of the KJV here is inconsistent with the general use of the Septuagint throughout this book, let it be considered as "poetic license," to allow introduction of material by the Church Fathers on Enoch.

50

THE LAMENT OF EVE

PART I

My children, my gifts from God, my children's children, gather round me. I am advanced in age and my voice is not strong. Listen to me, Adam, my beloved husband, you, who named me Eve, the source of life [46 (3:21)].*

Hearken, Seth, you who replaced my dear son, Abel, so cruelly slain by Cain, my firstborn.

Hearken Enos, Cainan, Maleleel, Jared, Mathusala and Lamech - all you good progeny who replaced Cain, the wanderer and all his evil generations [117].

Listen you wives and children of all my generations to an old woman lament and grieve.

Enoch is gone and to him I cannot speak, though he was good - no doubt the best of us - for God loved him and took him out of this life to keep this pure and favored one from knowing death [102 (5:24)].

My Lord, my God, my Creator made me. He formed me out of your father Adam's rib, a woman consubstantial with her husband [4, 13].

He loved us and nurtured us, and gave us equal dignity. He fashioned me to be a helpmate to my husband to nurture, in turn, the land and beasts and even the birds of the air - all creatures over which He gave us both dominion [4, 7, 9, 57].

In making us, He did not say "Let there be," as He had done in making all, including animals which He made first for

---

*Numbers in [ ] refer to numbered sections of Genesis and/or paragraphs of Church Fathers commentary in the Prologue.

51

us. My Lord deliberated with my Lord and said "Let Us make man according to Our image and likeness," to make us a special creation: to give us honor, dignity, dominion, and a mind to give him proper glory [1 (1:26), 2, 5].

How can I speak of this, my sin? But speak I must.

It cannot be that I should keep you all in ignorance of this immense calamity I, Eve, myself initiated. Perhaps by telling it, I can in a very small measure expiate my sin, or at the very least warn you and all my generations against an imitation and its consequences.

You see, beloved, God made us different from the animals in that he gave us all a rational soul [5]. He made us in His image.

Our dealings with the beasts which He had created for us were to be as masters, stewards, caretakers and the like.

The beasts look down towards the ground, but we humans stand and were made to look up at the heavens, to contemplate the spiritual [22].

In those good days we lived in Eden.

This was a paradise planted for us lovingly by God with all good things to exercise our stewardship.

He gave us heavenly food and nectar to sustain us, heavenly wisdom through Him, teaching of great knowledge, and every spiritual delight [38, 39].

And most of all and most important, my beloved - and listen to these words - He showered us with Love.

God is Love. He is and was and always will be our supreme and inexpressibly great Benefactor. He loves us all, and let us not ever have doubt of this, despite all ills and sufferings brought on by us, ourselves. For He is Love [68, 90, 105, 112].

This we do know: His love. But how can we, His crea-tures, fathom all the rest of Him? A glimpse we had of only the shadow of His grandeur and magnificence.

Imagine something grand, increase it to the total fulness of your high imagination, and even more: impossible it is for us to comprehend even a small part of God [2].

Our food and drink and our delight in Eden was just to do His will.

To love Him in return for His love gave warmth and meaning to our life.

A quiet joy, a sweet, inner stillness and contentment, serenity, and mutual respect and peacefulness pervaded both our souls.

In peace we lived with all the animals, and daily the birds sang for us the sweetest of melodies. The fragrance of beauteous flowers wafted at all times around us, and we knew nothing but contentment from God's abundant love.

We loved and helped each other and discussed and talked and sang the whole day long of our Creator's most abundant bounty.

We talked of our loving duties to the beasts and birds and fish and to all of nature, in imitation of our Maker's care.

We worked the earth to give the plants, the flowers and the trees the best soil and nourishment and rain and sun. The earthworms and bees and ants we cherished for their in-dustrious work within the scheme of nature.

Out feet trod heavenly grass, and the most succulent fruits of the trees composed a symphony of tastes and flavors in our mouths.

A celestial host of angels hovered about to lend their sweet voices as a great chorus to our glorying of Him, our greatest Benefactor.

Such beauty and such sweetness still lingers daily and strongly in my memory. Such bliss no one would wish to leave.

But leave we did, and all because of sin.

O God, my God! How can I speak of this, my shame? Help me, dear Father, as you have still led me all my life, despite my terrible unworthiness.

There was a tree in that delightful land, a noble tree, but looking not that much different from all the other trees. And yet this tree was special.

Our Father, our loving Benefactor, had singled out this tree, this one particular tree, as being out of bounds.

"You may eat," He said, "of every other tree in the garden, but not of this."

Those were His words. This was His commandment, a stricture for us both.

This, mark you, was the only thing forbidden by Him. The tree of life, also in the garden, of this we could eat, for we were then meant to be immortal [37, 75].

O grief! Most inconsolable grief! How can I ever justify denying my beloved Father this one request [85]?

It cannot, of course, be justified by human means, and let alone by sin-laden human means.

But once admitted, let me not shirk to continue the recital of this enormity: not only did I most deliberately rebel against my Lord's request, but even casually, as if of no consequence, I brushed His will aside [63].

Did I gainsay His will for a great purpose, or of necessity? No. How could I, His will is grounded in Omniscience [61].

I did it - O everlasting shame - because I listened to the serpent, that creature firmly in the grip and under the command of Satan [49, 50, 80].

And did this serpent speak great wisdom? No. How could he, prompted by the father of all lies?

He appealed only to those basest elements in me, those parts that, with my God-granted free will in His image, I was free to exercise or deny [21, 25, 35].

My children, let me now, with boldness and with full self-condemnation, proclaim my sin, my sin in all its exigencies:

I evidently did not love the Lord, my God, with my whole heart, with all my soul and with all my might, though He has created me and given me all I have.

I vainly set another, a mere serpent, the basest creature, up before Him, listened to its words and paid it more respect [51].

This beast, over which I was to have dominion, I set up as an idol of intelligence, and was deluded by its earthy blandishments and cunning.

I not only paid it more respect, but I betrayed to it the words and intent of God's injunction, and let it guide me in taking His holy name in vain [49].

I should have kept that day as a day of rest to enjoy my Father's good things, but notwithstanding, I went about inquisitively, looking at the forbidden tree.

My heavenly Father I failed miserably to honor. I failed even to ask Him to come to the spot and advise me how to argue with the snake [51].

Through this, my negligence, O my beloved children, I acknowledge truly that I have caused all of you to be subject to death, to imitation of your father, Adam and myself, and to be tempted to perpetuate the wages of our sin.

Instead of basking in the love of my Divine God, I had adulterous dealings with one who was His enemy.

I stole the only thing to steal, for all else was freely given to me by my divine Creator.

I confirmed the serpent's lie to my husband, Adam, emphasizing only the beauty of the fruit, and not the pride and covetousness that made me want to eat it, prompted by the devil's false promise that we would be like gods, knowing good and evil [52]. God had indeed prepared our immature and inexperienced minds with wisdom, and also with knowledge - especially of the evil of disobedience [38, 42A].

Together, Adam and I tried to cover up the consciousness of our misdeed, hiding even from God, who knows all things [60].

O woe, and everlasting woe is me!

We were expelled, and justly so, and caused to labor and to toil in pain and given a constant reminder by regret [70, 73, 87].

And we, and you too, by following our example, were condemned henceforth to end our lives in death. In His great foresight, our Lord forestalled all chances of our sinning in perpetuity by changing the location and the circumstances of our lives, making them transitory and mortal [64, 77].

In our appointed function - to cultivate and guard God's Paradise from evil, we had gravely failed. We did no longer have a right to occupy this place [58].

Another token of His love: though totally unworthy of His further loving care, He made us garments of skin and clothed us for our new life [68, 72].

In this temporal life we now have, you sin if you commit the same sins as I and Adam sinned, by imitation and by passions unbridled of your own. The Kingdom of God, the Paradise, that your father Adam and I left, is still perhaps available through God's love and mercy, though we must find, or be somehow shown the way to regain our way to it.

A blessed hope we see in Enoch, Jared's son, who pleased God so greatly that God took him, translated him, kept him from our own necessity to die. Where did He take him? We do not know. Suddenly he was not found. Could he be in our Eden, waiting for us to find a way to join him too? [102 (5:24), 110-116].

We ate, Adam and I, of the tree of knowledge, losing our virginal innocence by following our appetites. We had let evil set up an illusiory reality within our souls, distinct from the unchanging reality of God [55]. The temple of our souls could not contain them both.

How did that knowledge affect us in our lives? Through God's justice, we learned and observed from our firstborn sons, Cain and Abel. Cain was bad and Abel was good.

O the grief of a mother to tell of this: to have nurtured her sons and watched them grow and wished them every good! O, the just punishment of our God and Maker to make us see the going astray of our beloved firstborn, Cain, to let us watch the patient care and stewardship of Abel with his flock, and to reflect on the promise of such a son, with so much love of God and beast.

God knew their hearts - as He knows every heart of man - and He accepted Abel's offering and scorned that of Cain. Why did He so distinguish? Listen to the account.

Abel was a keeper of sheep, but Cain was a tiller of the ground.

Their father and I - in much renewed gratitude - had taught them to revere our God and to bring Him offerings to demonstrate their love.

My own gratitude as a mother was so great at Cain's birth, God's token of His continuing love - despite our terrible transgressions - that I most greatly praised Him that I had gained a man through God [86 (4:1), 89, 90].

And in His great mercy, he granted me another, Abel, and all of you here now.

Cain, then, after some time, brought the fruits of the earth, a sacrifice to the Lord [91].

Abel, as his offering, brought of the firstborn of his sheep and of his fatlings [86 (4:4)].

And God looked upon Abel and his gifts, but Cain and his sacrifices he regarded not.

Abel, you see, had greatly and sincerely honored God by giving Him of his very best: his "firstborn" and even the very special ones of these, the fatlings [92].

Did Cain bring his "firstfruits"? Alas no, he brought whatever came to hand, casually and without thought, or - God forgive me for thinking this - perhaps even the cast-off fruit [93, 95].

Casually, I said. O shades of my own casual attitude in disobeying God!

Cain brought his offering "after some time," as if it were not the most joyful and immediate thing that he could do: to offer his best to God [86 (4:3), 98].

Abel, my son, moreover, was not a casual sheep-herder, but a good pastor, caring for the good of those under his charge. Cain, alas, was casual, unthinking in all his ways. He tilled the earth, but failed to cultivate it, nourish it, make it bring forth its best yield [98].

But God knows all, my children, and He is just.

He put sorrow into Cain's heart to bring him to his senses, yet at the same time He acknowledged the dignity of Cain's own status as the firstborn with rights to rule his brother [86 (4:14), 94].

But Cain, alas, listened to the promptings of his own bitterness at this encounter with refusal. How can I point a finger at my son's failure to amend his attitude, when I am the chief sinner by example? You see already, my dear children, how he imitated me in my great sin.

O Lord, have mercy on us all!

And Cain rose up against Abel, his brother, and slew him. O the memory of this bloody deed, with Adam, their father and I watching them on the plain! What frightful punishment for all our sins! [96].

What horror we felt at this, our very first sight of death! [96, 105].

How could the God of Love ever forgive our many sins? And how could we ever be restored to our most pristine state after such horrible, vile deeds?

Cain, Adam and I never saw again. God cursed him, and he left the presence of His Creator, and made himself a fugitive and a vagabond on earth. His progeny are lost to us [99, 104].

My children, you must guard against denying yourself the presence of God within your life, be it casually or with intent. Know that to have God is to have all and to lose Him is to have nothing worthy of any name.

But - God be praised - in His great love and mercy, Adam and I did conceive again, and I bore Seth. God raised me up another seed instead of Abel, whom Cain slew. God the Almighty can raise whom He will and He was gracious to us both. May He be as gracious to all of you to resurrect life from death [96, 105, 106].

Seth was after Adam's own form and after his own image [102 (5:3), 105].

My beloved husband, Adam, was created by God in comeliness and with the intent of enjoying the supreme good: attachment to God and conjunction with Him through love and in life everlasting. The same was intended for me after my creation as his helpmate [21, 32, 35, 36, 39].

After the loss of our first children, Seth was our substitute, to help to bring us back to this initial form and image.

Indeed Seth, you had a son and called his name Enos: hoping to call on the name of the Lord God.

My children, my beloved, we have so sadly failed in our quest to regain this image: His image in all our thoughts and deeds, to shape His likeness in our souls [3, 56].

We seek only pleasure and the things of this alluring world. We forget God and His love. We allow ourselves to be governed by the passions of pride, greed, lust and judgment, anger and bitterness. We do not struggle daily and strive as we ought, to get back to our pristine being [44].

We put God last instead of first. We offer not our first-fruits: we offer nothing to Him in thanksgiving for our being. We have all sinned and strayed away from His abiding love and mercy.

Let us make daily offerings to Him, though His of His own we offer: be it time, labor, products, alms or just our love.

Let us strive mightily to call on God to send His Spirit down upon our sacrifice.

If you give God of your best: if you are open to receive God's grace and work obediently to collaborate with Him, He surely will bless your effort and increase its fruit [5, cf. 1 Cor. 3:6, 7].

Let us petition Him. Let us pray fervently for Him to give us grace and strength to overcome our negligent ways through our own God-given free will. Let us beseech Him to send someone to show us the way.

We must keep faith and know the potential of good: of God's own likeness growing in us.

We must have purity and keep ourselves untainted by any evil growing up around us.

We must be ready to receive His will and His commandments like soil receptive to seed, rain and nourishment.

We must keep hope in patience and endurance through drought or rains, sickness or health, steadfast in our love of God.

And we must know, above all, with the guidance of such who call on God and glorify His name, to know the real, the true, the good from falsehood and deception. For only the pure and real can live with God and He in them [116A].

Lamech, if you have a son, call him Noah - Rest, Relief - from this evil state into which we have directed ourselves. Let God help us to wash away all evil, and let Noah, your hoped-for son, be good, to start anew a life for all our future generations.

Give us descendants, O God, who will show the way to right sacrifice and righteousness in all things.

And give me a great-great-granddaughter, my beloved God, who will be as I was not: totally obedient and submissive to God in all things, worthy to bring a new birth and a new life to man in God [82].

And pray that God may restore the bones of Adam and me and all of you in some miraculous way from death to life. Amen.

PART II

REFLECTIONS ON GOD'S WISDOM

I have told you, children, how often our Lord imparted to us the benefit of His wisdom [38]. Would that we had listened then to all He tried to teach us in connection with our being as He had created us with free will, changeability, our purpose of stewardship of the earth, respect for His primacy of dominion, and why it was we were forbidden the fruit of that one tree [42A].

In old age my memory of "childhood" times is stronger, and I will now give you of my remembrance.

Would that we both had heeded all his words back then, and reflected before breaking His commandment. Adam and I would not have visited this life of suffering and toil on all of you. Forgive us.

Our hope in this our transient life we now live is in the very difference between man and God. For God is absolute, unchanging, and we are changeable. We know, through His great wisdom that even by our creation we were changed from nothingness to being. And all that is produced is subject also to change [15, 25, 35]. Through beneficial change in this our mortal life, we can still grow towards perfection (cf. Mt. 5:48).

In warning Adam and me not to partake of that one tree, God wanted to teach us that we were alterable and changeable and immature, and should beware in order to remain in our same good and most pure condition [37, 42A].

The first change after our fall from Paradise was in the manner of procreation. In Paradise, Adam and I were like the angels, together in love and thought and spirit, but all enraptured by our adoring love of God. No thought of physical

62

proximity in love did cross our minds. The warmth of God's love was all in all [88].

The angels multiplied, created as Adam was, or by mysterious means, by the almighty hand of God [14, 16, 18, 19, 20, 27, 88]. But after we had lost the all-embracing warmth of Paradise, Adam and I clung to each other for love and warmth and solace, and within His foreknowledge, grace and almighty plan, our Lord Creator's providence allowed us the use of our built-in means to help Him generate and continue the creation of mankind.

God, you see, my children, knows all things beforehand, yet He does not predetermine all things. For He knows beforehand those things that are in our power, but He does not predetermine them. He predetermines only those things not in our power, in accordance with His prescience [26].

In making us in His image, our Lord endowed us with free will. But herein lay our problem and our challenge and our power, causing our heavenly Teacher to warn us to beware that we were changeable.

We had the free will and power to preserve our natural state in Paradise by persevering in the contemplation of all good, or to be lured by passions: pride, covetousness, vainglory, by laxity, and many such corruptions, to fall into both sin and death [21, 25, 35].

You excuse us, saying we were not properly aware beforehand of these results of good and evil? But alas, we knew what it meant to obey or disobey our Lord's commandment, instructed by God's teaching [38].

You say we are all still alive, not dead? But God said "Earth thou art, and to earth thou shalt return." We all have become liable to death, and from that moment - banished by our own deed from His grace - we are dead in effect [71, 81]. We both saw well in Abel, our son, the fact of death.

Virtue, we know, is a gift from God implanted in our nature. He, God, Himself is the source and cause of all good, and without His cooperation and help we cannot will or do any good thing [26].

God, being all good, did not create sin in human nature or in me. It was my own transgression of His divine law that resulted in corrupting my own nature, and it is your sins that serve to corrupt yours [23].

My progeny, listen to me, who understands only too well from experience of error.

Do not, I beseech you all, pit your free will against our Lord's commandments. He tested us with the tree, Adam and me, to see if we would preserve the dignity of the soul by reasonably acknowledging our Creator and observing His command, and thereby share eternal blessedness and live to all eternity.

But if, instead, we should subject the soul to the mortal body, trading our true dignity to base earthly things and senseless beasts, allurements and desires, we would be liable to death, corruption and compelled to labor throughout a miserable life.

We were created, you see, to be intermediate, standing between God and matter. Destined we were, if proved obedient and ever mindful of His loving will, to have dominion over all things material, if we could keep our souls from being drawn, through pride and base passions, to focus exclusively on the material world, away from God [29, 30, 31].

God gave us a body, soul and spirit: the body as instrument for the soul and for our procreation.

The soul includes our mind, our reason, memory, will, and most especially our heart, all these comprising our inner person.

This inner person must be cultivated, helped by grace to grow into the likeness of our loving God, to do His will and help us fit into His kingdom.

Not by our own efforts can we do this, but we must stretch our soul, our spirit, our tamed bodies towards God and beg His help.

Do not let your spirit be tempted and stained with evil spirits: malice, envy, anger, impurity and suchlike passions, but let it seek the Holy Spirit of our God.

Let God be formed in you, but God will only dwell within a temple of great purity [3, 5, 13, 116A].

Your father, Adam, gave names to all the animals, the birds and brute beasts in token of dominion. He named even me *Zoë*, the mother of life and spoke prophetically about the relationship of man and woman [38, 24 (2:24), 46 (3:21)].

In the beginning none of the wild beasts caused fear in either Adam or myself. They recognized human direction and dominion, as with tame animals even now [48]. But when we were banished from Paradise, the beasts no longer did submit to us [66]. Indeed we have neglected our care also of plants and trees and all the living things created by God since we burdened ourselves with all our passions.

God meant us to be free from passion, sinless, to be free from care [23, 32]. Our life was not meant to be our own, but that of God, in ever greater likeness not to brutes but to our Author.

God is eternal and beasts and earthly things are transient. To separate our will and actions from God is to expell ourselves from immortality and to die [71].

Despite this knowledge and this consoling memory, we yearn and thirst, Adam and I, for our Edenic blessed natural state, when we lived naked, innocent, and without shame. We lived on earth as if we were in heaven, trouble-free, angelic, needing no shelter. Our home was spiritual then, cultivating divine thoughts, living in sweet simplicity, a life free from all things artificial, in contemplation of our heavenly Father in whom we found all joy and gladness.

We hallowed His holy name in His kingdom, did His holy will and He filled all our needs.

In our present corruption, I pray that all of you may one day worthily call Him Father, His heavenly kingdom will come to us again, that He will forgive us our trespasses, that He may teach us to forgive those who sin against us, lead us away from temptations, and deliver us from the evil one [49].

As long as man was holy and passionless, he had no need of law [36].

But now we know we do need our Lord's commandments.

The loving God, wanting to teach us that we have a Creator who produced us and all visible realities, wished also to reveal His own dominion and preeminence. Although our Lord entrusted us with his earthly creation, He knew we could be prone to fall into pride, exaggerate our importance as humans, and to regard visible things and even ourselves as self-sufficient [55].

And what of me, Eve, created as one meet to help Adam, with whom I was of equal dignity? [51] How did I fall so low as to become a temptress of my husband because of the promptings of a mere beast, or rather of basest Satan?

Was it not from this same pride and wish to seem sufficient and - God forgive me - greater than my Creator? [52]

What can I say of God's justice and reprimand when He, my Lord, sentenced me to be submissive henceforth to Adam, my dear husband? [46 (3:17)].

Adam, too, was found at fault and punished. And we proceeded into life and into its struggles together "of one flesh," and yet still of equal honor, and each giving the other reverence and respect [57]. We were both wrong [57, 80]. We were both slaves to sin. May we now serve each other in humility and love of God [43].

And this same honor is to be accorded, too, to us as parents. As you, my children, became parents, you understood the mystery and the suffering of this great function [45].

But you wives, never forget the role of a good woman to her own husband and in this world. As I was given to Adam, she too can be a divine gift. Instead of leading him astray, as I did, let her rather be an inspiration for all good things. Let her be his support, to lend him courage, solace, sustenance, support, and even gentle leadership, if need be, into the spiritual realm. Let her act as an example of meekness, patience, steadfastness and faith to him and to their children and of the great power of love [40, 41, 42]. Let her be an example and inspiration also in how we all can overcome our baser natures.

Know that the attributes of our nature similar to those of beasts - given to them for self-preservation - can easily in us become the passions: greed, gluttony, vainglory, lust, envy, anger, and so on. And yet if reason and faith assume sway over base emotions, each passion can be transmuted to a form of virtue: anger produces courage; terror caution, fear obedience, hatred aversion from vice; and the power of love the desire for divine love and beauty [17].

Fear, terror, hatred and suspicion, all these are the fruit of sin. Before our grave sin, we knew no active fear nor shame. Only thereafter we hid and feared to face our God [60].

Active respect for God's direction, belief in His good word, and dread of the punishment likely to follow the eating of the fruit, as taught by Him, were the emotions common to us in Paradise [49].

O God, my God, when I think of the great and all-encompassing love you had and still show for us, I weep great hot and heavy tears [68].

Before our Fall, we lived, Adam and I and God's presence in our lives, in perfect love and harmony. But as soon as we listened to God's adversary and had eaten of the fruit of the knowledge of good and evil, we had the boldness, the audacity, the arrogance, the gracelessness to judge and blame others rather than ourselves. Confess I must that our feeble attempt to imitate God our Maker and think ourselves ready for true contemplation, produced only cowardly recriminations, quarrels, enmity, entirely untempered by love and mercy [42A, 53, 64].

The deceiver was the first heretic in judging God's motives [46 (3:6), 49]. Adam blamed me for listening and handing him the fruit, and even God he blamed [46 (3:13), 64]. And I blamed Adam for his indifference. He listened to my dialogue with the deceiver and failed to stop me, breaking God's law himself as well in accepting the fruit from my hand [53].

But our awareness of these things, alas, has come too late. Our eyes are opened now and well do we now know our loss of communion with our benevolent Father [66].

Beware, my children, that same adversary who deceived us is still a foe lurking within us all [56]. Know also, my beloved, that true knowledge, omniscience creates the ability to judge. And we on earth are not omniscient. False knowledge, linked with pride, leads merely to false and futile judgments, and to a lack of peace on earth and also within our souls.

And if we imitate God's adversary, relying on falseness and vain imaginings, God will withdraw His grace. He will withdraw His health from us, His wisdom, beauty, blessedness and leave us weak, ugly, sick, and wretched [80].

Listen, my progeny, to the expression of my profound regret. Hear of my ingratitude, my deliberate turning away from God and His consequent withdrawal from my soul, leaving me full of sorrow. But help me, help all of us to turn again to God [61].

For there is hope. This surely we must believe. We know, you see, that after our great sin, God still saw extenuating circumstances [61] and sought us in the garden. We hid in fear, but God sought us in His great love [46 (3:10)]. Even in His action in expelling us and prescribing our present hard life for us, He gave us an opportunity for penance and perhaps eventual return [78].

But this return requires great effort and cooperation with God's will [12]. Our Father told us that we, Adam and I, were made in His image. What does this mean? God is holy, passionless and sinless. He, God, Himself is uncreate and unchanging, absolute, but we are created, made by God. Therein does lie a difference.

For when we were created - changed from nothing to that which we are - we then remained susceptible to change [35]. Moreover, in His image, God gave us free will. Now therein lies the effort. For free will can lead us away from the likeness of God's holiness to sin and passion, as it has. Or it could have been used to live within God's way, according to the will and purposes of our most loving Father. This way, this likeness, this perfection we must strive ever to attain for our fulfilment, restoration and mastery of death, and for our return to His affectionate embrace.

By His great mercy, perhaps we can still look on this time, our time on earth, marked by this very characteristic of change built into it, as our "acceptable time" to gain this end [1 Cor. 6:12, Rom. 8:23].

But this is a task too great for me, the sinful one. Too long, already, have I lived and become used to the corruption of this world. And you, my children - God forgive me - have been besmirched through imitation, as He foreknew [67].

Our Lord, God has removed His grace from us, because we have turned away from Him [34].

When Seth was born in Adam's own form and image as he had been early in Paradise [102 (5:3), 105, 108] we both hoped this sign of God's love would bring us back into His grace.

Seth, too, hoped his son Enos would call on the Lord's name [108]. You know we chose these names because of our great hope [96, 109].

Enoch was born and greatly pleased the Lord, and God did take him to Himself [110, 111].

Lamech, you must have a son and call him Noah [rest, relief]. Teach him to lead a holy life and hope that we all may be washed clean and start anew.

Always be aware, my children, of the importance of the names: for memory, for example, for gratitude, and hope and guidance for the future [96, 97, 108, 109, 114].

Mark well, beloved, these things we hope for can only happen by God's grace. But well we know His providence is great: the care He takes over existing things as our Creator and Provider [33].

I weep great tears, O Lord, when I remember your benevolence, your loving care [54, 55], and how I have grieved my loving Father [81, 85].

Well I remember how even in the depth of our shame and nakedness, You showed Your pity, Lord, and made us simple garments of skin [46 (3:22), 72]. With stern love, like a parent, You taught us by Your actions to lead a fruitful and austere life [73].

Let us always give praise to God for all His providence.

Praise Him even for His will, expressing severity, discipline, abstinence and sacrifice.

Praise Him for our very lives.

Praise Him for all His guidance in our abysmal ignorance, arrogance and daily falls [107].

Let us at all times and in every way offer our firstfruits to Him: our first hour and our last, our talents, and all the gifts and fruits of life, joy, sun, rain and beneficence showered upon our sinful souls [92].

Thine of Thine own we offer unto Thee, O Lord.

May we at all times demonstrate our love for Him through offerings, sacrifice and praise, to show our loving intention towards Him [95].

Though sharing one flesh in marriage, and united in love and honor to our parents, let all of us at all times give Him primacy. And let no jealousy or resentment prevail for this, His first place, for know He loves us all: all thoughts and actions directed to and through Him will be forever for all our good.

Forgive me, children, I preach these things, the sinful one, but know they come with love to you from my own sad experience.

They come from my memory and from my daily weeping over our great loss of God's grace.

O God, at dawn I rise to You. My soul hungers and thirsts for You.

My soul mourns for that Edenic closeness we once had. Restore us all, O Lord.

Come to us, Lord. Visit this earth and help us, heal us, save us from all our pitiful corruption [56].

You made me a woman, Lord. Lord help me through a daughter, a woman meet to be a helpmate for all mankind, willing and able to intercede for us at Your almighty throne.

Create her, Lord, with all the qualities I lacked in my great sin: humility, obedience, purity, steadfast faith in You. And let her bear One in Your divine image and of Your essence to be our holy Savior [82].

EPILOGUE - PART I

LETTER TO A SPIRITUAL DAUGHTER[1]:

LESSONS IN DIVINE AND CHRISTIAN LOVE

According to your wish I am writing this, my daughter, I, the humble Callistratus.

1. As all realities of the universe, with their quality and effects, are only symbols of spiritual reality, so also is worldly love. That which people on earth have called "love" in reality is only a pale symbol of true divine love.

2. All that exists can divide itself into uncreate and created. God is uncreate; everything else is created. And love is uncreate: uncreate and eternal. For love is not just an attribute of God but the name of God - one of the names of God - and the plenitude of divine being. That is also how it has been said "God is love" (1 Jn. 4:8).

3. It has also been said that God is the Truth and the Word. Wonderful is this Slavic word *istina* - which perfectly designates Him who is forever true. "I am that I am;" in short: I am the same, unchanging ... And the Word, is the expression of the hidden God. And just as Truth and Word are eternally in God and are God, so is Love. And just as Word speaks for itself: "I am the Alpha and Omega, the Beginning and the End," so Love can say of itself: "I am the Alpha and Omega."

4. As love, God manifests Himself to mankind through the revelation of the Holy Trinity in unity, Father and Son and Holy Spirit - one God - and through the incarnation of God the Word. In the Old Testament, the Testament of the Law, God is only indicated as the Holy Trinity. So also Love placed itself without calling attention to itself among the many other commandments of the law (cf. Deut 6:5, Ex. 19:18). The world was not ready for the reception of doctrine on the Holy Trinity, and consequently, not on

---

1. This letter is Chapter Six of KASSIANA, from The Collected Works of Bishop Nikolai Velimirovich, Book XII. The letter is from Archimandrite Callistratus, Abbot of Mileševo Orthodox Monastery in Bosnia-Herzogovina, to his spiritual daughter, the nun Kassiana. Before her tonsure, she had blasphemed God in despair over her unsightliness as a hunchback and its ramifications. The abbot teaches her about divine love and brings her back to God to serve Him through her love of children. This version © Johanna Manley.

Love. But these two are indivisible. The commandment of love, the last among the commandments of the Old Testament has become the first in the New Testament.

5. In the pagan world, faith in a trinity existed, but not in the Divinity, holy and unique. The people of India have believed, and still believe in the Trimurti, that is in three supreme gods, one of whom is Shiva, the destroyer of all that the other two, Vishnu and Brahma, create. In Egypt belief is likewise in a triad, but as in a family with bodily love, out of whom Osiris and Isis generate a son, Horus, who kills Osiris, which dissolves this monstrous marriage. Before Christ, men were able with their own spirit and effort to create great civilizations for all continents of the earth, but it was not possible to arrive at a proper concept of God as the Holy Trinity in Unity, consequently not of God as Love.

6. Islam, though one of the relatively advanced religions, in no way endured the doctrine of God as the Holy Trinity. In the Koran this doctrine is ridiculed. And in the Mosque of Omar in Jerusalem this command is carved on the wall: "True believers, know that Allah does not have a Son". And precisely since according to that religion God has no Son, in the Koran nothing is said of God's love but only of God's justice and mercy. Although Mohammed took his doctrines out of the Old Testament, he did not read the words of the Almighty: "Shall I bring to the birth, and not cause to bring forth? saith the Lord: shall I cause to bring forth, and shut the womb?" (Isa. 66:9). And not only Mohammed but also the ancient Aryans and the modern Unitarians.

7. Know and remember, my daughter, the mystery of the Holy Trinity is the intimate mystery of the divine Being. This inner mystery God could not reveal to the people without law, nor through the law, neither through man nor through the great prophets. Nor is it announced through the chosen prophets clearly enough and incontrovertibly, regarding the descent to earth of His Son in the Incarnation, through whom "the earth shall be full of the knowledge of the Lord, as the waters cover the sea" (Isa. 11:9, Hab. 2:14). And the most important knowledge which the Son revealed, would be the glorious knowledge of God as the Holy Trinity, one of each of whose names is Love.

8. The eternal Father loves the Son and the Holy Spirit. The eternal Son loves the Father and the Holy Spirit. The eternal Spirit loves the Father and the Son. All in inconceivable unity, indivisible and without confusion. All incorporeal and spiritual. And as such from everlasting to everlasting, without beginning and without end, without change, without

74

diminution or increase, without influence of time and space, and despite any exterior occurrence.

9. To imagine God without the Son is the same as if one imagined God without love. For all love requires an object for its love. You know, daughter, that when any of the people say: "I love", we immediately and logically ask: "whom do you love?" Whom, therefore would God the Father have loved in eternity, before creating the world, if He had not had the Son as object of His love? This would mean that He did not know to love, or that Love had not had a part in His essence before the world was created as the object of His Love. But that again would indicate, that God by the creation of the world, would have acquired something that He did not have before, and that thereby He had been changed. That is senseless and illogical and contradictory to the Holy Scripture of God, which has revealed from on high that "in God there is no change."

10. Whoever does not believe in the begetting of God the Son from God the Father, cannot in any manner give to God the name of Father. If they nevertheless call Him thus, they are not speaking the truth. For to whom is He a Father if He does not have a Son? The name Father could perhaps be honorary or titular, as if children somewhere addressed some older man Father. But if someones says: God is the Father of all men, do we not immediately answer: 'God is the Creator, but not the Father of all people'? He created all mankind, but He did not generate men. If a blacksmith has sons and forged some ploughs, has he not formed distinctions between his own children and his product? No one may, without lying, name God Father without recognizing His eternally begotten Son; Who solely has the power to make the transformation from having been begotten to having created. The Apostle of Christ says decisively: "Whoever denieth the Son, the same hath not the Father: but he that acknowledgeth the Son hath the Father also" (1 Jn. 2:23; 4:15-16).

11. In the second paragraph of our Creed we confess our faith "in one God - Lord Jesus Christ, Son of God, only-begotten, begotten of the Father before all ages, begotten but not created." Oh how we ought to be exalted by the Holy Church Fathers, who emphasized and confirmed this truth! Otherwise we would have been liars when we spoke of the Father without speaking of the Son. For if the Father does not have a Son, whose Father He is, why would He also have called Himself Father? And all our speaking of Love would have been only some nostalgic poem without real justification.

12. God as Love explains Himself solely through God as the Holy Trinity. In that is the secret key to love, my daughter. Keep this continually in mind. And believe the words of the great Isaac the Syrian: "Love is the sweetness of life." But I add: and stronger than death.

13. When we speak of love in the Holy Trinity, we continually think in our intellect that God is spirit and the love existing in Him is all spiritual. The Father loves the Son so strongly, that all is for the Son: and the Son loves the Father so strongly, that all is for the Father; and the Holy Spirit so loves that all is for the Father and the Son. This is the Son bearing witness of God in words: "I am in the Father and the Father is in Me" (Jn. 14:10). Equally, the Son is in the Holy Spirit and the Holy Spirit in the Son. The Scripture witnesses regarding the risen Christ and the disciples: "He breathed on them, and saith unto them, Receive ye the Holy Spirit" (Jn. 20:22). One can only give what is carried within oneself.

14. The characteristic of love, my daughter, is that it desires to identify itself profoundly with the person of the beloved. Such is the ardent love the Father has towards the Son, that He desires to sink and lose Himself in the Son. And conversely. Such is the love of the Holy Spirit with respect to the Father and the Son. Yet by an inevitable indispensability, each person remains as is. Therefore also it is said of the Holy Trinity "indivisible - without confusion." It is indivisible, for It is one in essence and of the same loving energy; It is without confusion, since each Person by His particular hypostasis is individual. It is a triple flame of being, of life and of love. From that magnificent divine fire of love we also kindle our small, blessed candles of earthly love, which flicker and smoke, damped by faintness of breath. But what the three Persons carry in full force and undivided, that is the action of love of each Person towards the other two. For each of them longs, out of love, to magnify and glorify the remaining two Persons of the Holy Trinity. That was made clear by the word of the Son of God: "My Father is greater than I" (Jn. 14:28).

15. The love in one person by himself is not love but self-love and selfishness. This is precisely why Mohammed also did not mention love in connection with Allah but only righteousness and mercy. Love between two persons quickly cools and turns into sadness. This is why, in the Old Testament, barrenness was considered a curse ... Love fully complete is love of three together. On earth this is so in consequence of the way it is in heaven. It is no wonder how the number three plays an enormous part in all products of the Creator, unique and in Trinity.

16. Love has not arisen from earth, but is granted from heaven. St. Cassian said: " Love belongs exclusively to God, and those men who have renewed in themselves the image and the likeness of God." Conscious love refers to the conscious person and not to a principle or an idea nor to an impersonal creation, but to personhood. Where there is no reciprocity in love, there is no love. But a principle or an idea or a creation, be it of God or of man, cannot love us, though we may love it. Of that love we are not speaking, but of the love that is from person to person and which is "indivisible and without confusion."

17. Only the perfect person, with a perfect conscience, a perfect mind, and perfect power, can have perfect love. Such a person is our God. What every man eagerly desires for his person is therefore that which exists in the person of his Creator. What all people value - love above all - that is therefore what the Creator is - Love. And so it has been from time immemorial to today and unto ages of ages.

18. It is always the inferior that is proved by the superior, but not conversely. In this way the human being evidences a higher existence, a higher power, and higher intelligence. A certain European philosopher has said: "I think, therefore I am." And indeed that word of his is proclaimed to the world as something great ...

If God does not exist as certainly more intelligent than I, then it is evident that I do not exist, or that I am only some temporary apparition, a ghost fluttering out of the stirred-up dust and formed in an instant, in order only to fall again into the same dust, aimlessly and without leaving a trace. Just the same is love. If love does not exist in God and does not come from God, then it is only some sentimental lust which men have used as a narcotic, in order to be somewhat foolishly alleviated of the great absurdity of life.

19. "God is love; and he that dwelleth in love dwelleth in God and God in him" (1 Jn. 4:16). Ages and generations of men have waited to hear those enlightening and enlivening words as guiding stars like the star of Bethlehem. The apostle said, heard, felt and repeated it as he had received it from his Lord. The God of truth and of love is the everlasting God. He has no contact or union with "agreements" of lies and hate. By this revelation, Christ has overturned all polytheistic pantheons which human phantasy have placed at the feet of egalitarian gods, good and bad.

20. It is not easy to comprehend why God has created the worlds: first the incorporeal angels, then afterwards the physical, material, with man at the top. If the trinitarian God is perfect and sufficient in Himself, in the

77

fullness of life, love and glory, why has He created the worlds which are inferior to Himself? (We say, inferior to Himself, for no one can create anything equal to himself. Beget yes: God the Father begot the Son equal to
Himself; and man begets children equal to himself in being and essence).
The Church - and only the Church - gives the answer: in His bountiful love,
which exists in Him, God created all worlds, invisible and visible, through
His Son, the only-begotten, in order to please His Son. Was it for the sake
of the Son's pleasure, or for His need? We do not say this. For God
amusement is not needed. His trinitarian love exceeds all joy, amusement
and all delectable celebration. One who is perfect is self-sufficient and has
no need for anything, for he contains all in himself.

21. With boundless love towards the Father, the Son wanted to please
the Father by this which was created for Him: more sons for Himself and
more brothers, lower than Himself, but bonded in love to Him by adoption.
And in the eternal Council, the Father and the Holy Spirit are in accord
with the Son for the creation of the worlds through love of the Son. And so
it was that all came into being that came into being through the Son. "And
all things were made by Him" (Jn. 1:3). And the Son of God is also called
the Logos of God, or the Word of God, that is, the Image of God (cf. Col.
1:15-17); yes, God's poem, by which is made known the majesty and glory
and wisdom and love of God ...

22. Having taken the initiative in creating, the Son has also taken the
responsibility for the created worlds before His eternal Council. In addition to that, He has given voluntary agreement to offer Himself as a
sacrifice when and if that should be needed as an innocent and pure lamb,
foreordained for sacrifice "before the foundation of the world" (1 Peter
1:20). And so began an incomparable epic poem of poems: an epic of the
creation of the world, its temptation, fall, resurrection and renewal. All this
as it has been told and foretold. And all with one single and unique motive:
love. For God is Love and for Him there is no other motivation besides
love, my daughter, who loves God and is beloved by Him.

23. And the Son of God created innumerable heavenly intelligences
from archangels to angels, incorporeal spirits close to God. He created
them in the image of God, powerful and very beautiful. And He gave them
free will. But the sole God did not abuse free will! One of the great angels,
Satan - or Lucifer - did use for evil the free will given to him, and he
removed himself an endless distance from the presence of God with his
legions of adherents, and cast himself into Hades, to the outermost darkness.

EPILOGUE I: LESSONS IN DIVINE AND CHRISTIAN LOVE

However, the Word of God, in agreement with the eternal Council, created the man Adam, and the woman Eve out of his body, and placed them in Paradise. But Satan deceived them through the agency of the serpent, and they sinned against God. God did not wish to pardon Satan the sin, for he had sinned in too close proximity to God. But God did will to pardon Adam, for man was deceived by Satan. God willed to pardon Adam but not without repentance on his part and appropriate sacrifice. And the Son of God, the Lamb of God, went to His immolation for the sake of Adam's temptation and his generation. All out of love. And for justice, you say? Yes, to satisfy justice, but justice is included in love.

24. So "in this was manifested the love of God towards us, because God sent His only begotten Son into the world, that we might live through Him ...not that we loved God, but that He loved us, and sent His Son to be a propitiation for our sins" (1 Jn. 4:9-10). Primarily He thereby shows His love for us, so therefore He looks towards our demonstrating our love for Him. Do we or do we not desire - that depends on us - either the eternal reward of faithful love or again the eternal torment of forsaken love. For outside of the temporal, in eternity, time does not exist - all is eternal, be it joy or be it torment.

25. In Jesus Christ the Son, God is revealed as love "which passeth all understanding." He, through whom the Holy Trinity has created the world, demonstrates Himself as a man of the flesh, so that the love of the Holy Trinity is manifested to mankind, a love thus far unknown to the world. How did it demonstrate itself? In a manner in which only great love is not shy, as it shows itself for the sake of the salvation of the beloved: by humiliation and kenosis, by service, suffering, and finally by the supreme sacrifice.

26. In the stories and ballads set to rhythm we read how those with love for their intended deliver themselves gladly to suffering for their beloved; sometimes even to death. But the betrothed had been worthy of their love and sacrifice in the manner described by poets. However, the sinless and pure Christ endured humiliation, suffering and a horrible death, not for some innocent, faithful and good virgin, but for sinners and the dissolute, for murderers, liars, thieves, abductors, bandits, perjurers and godless, for men with polluted and malodorous souls, who smelled of deadly corruption, and who were dead before death. "For scarcely for a righteous man will one die ... but God commendeth His love towards us, in that, while we were yet sinners, Christ died for us" (Rom. 5:6-8). Is this not the kind of love that passes all understanding?

27. "Love seeketh not her own," says the Apostle, teaching his disciples by example (1 Cor. 13:5). All His words and deeds the Son of God ascribed to the Father. "I speak not of Myself: but the Father that dwelleth in Me" (Jn. 14:10) "I speak all that I have heard from Him" (cf. Jn. 14:10). "I have come down from heaven not to do My own will, but the will of the Father who sent Me" (cf. Jn. 4:34, 5; 5:30). "My meat is to do the will of Him who sent Me and finish His work" (cf. Jn. 4:34, 5:36). "As the Father gave Me commandment, so I do" (Jn. 14:31). "All that you see that I have is love for the Father" (cf. Jn. 16:15). Look at the Gospel of St. John. O when will the sons of men so love their parents! So, the Son renounces His will and attributes all to the Father. Neither does He seek His own glory, but His Father's. Again, on another side too the Father loves the Son "and all I have shown Him." Nor does the Father judge anyone "but hath committed all judgment unto the Son" (Jn. 5:22). And moreover: "The Father loves the Son and has given all things into His hands" (cf. Jn. 13:3).

28. In love, the Father and the Son and also the Holy Spirit participate in full measure. By the Holy Spirit was enabled the birth of the Son from the Virgin Mary without a man. The Holy Spirit revealed Himself, being seen as a dove at the baptism of Christ. Full of the Holy Spirit, Jesus returned from the Jordan. By the Holy Spirit Jesus cast out evil demons from men. The Holy Spirit descended on the apostles at Pentecost. "God appeared in the flesh, justified by the Spirit." "As many as are led by the Spirit of God, they are the sons of God" (Rom. 8:14). One unpardonable blasphemy is blasphemy against the Holy Spirit (cf. Mt. 12:31). The spirit of life, power, wisdom, truth, prayer, peace, joy, comfort dwells in those who believe in Christ as in His temple. It continues the work of Christ uniting the faithful into one dedicated body which is the Church, "the pillar and ground of the truth" (1 Tim. 3:15) And above all "the love of God is shed abroad in our hearts by the Holy Spirit which is given unto us" (Rom. 5:5).

29. Accordingly when it is said: "God is love," by this is said that the entire Holy Trinity is Love. The Father is Love and the Son is Love and the Holy Spirit is Love. The source and the original countenance of love between the angels and men, the source who was giving of Himself without ceasing and receiving without enrichment.

30. Listen, daughter, to those words of unspoken bravery, which are characteristic only of love. Out of love, the Son of God humiliated Himself, served, taught, healed, fed, strengthened, straightened, gladdened, suffered, was in distress, forgave, and died. "The Son of man came not to be ministered unto, but to minister, and to give His life a ransom for many" (Mt. 20:28). When serving, He served with rejoicing; when sacrificing Himself,

He sacrificed voluntarily, not worrying about Himself, but looking constantly with an everlasting ardent love towards the heavens, at those two other Persons of the Trinity. That is the simple existence of eternal love in the Son. That is the natural way also of men who have love. Because of this, Nilus of Sinai says: "With pain you have acquired divine love: that all will become easy to do and to maintain. But where there is no love, there is no repose." And all becomes difficult and impossible.

31. Love is joy; the price of love is sacrifice. Love is life; the price of love is death.

32. He who loves earthly wealth, power and glory, pitilessly hounds other men to serve his senseless "love." And sacrificing for this "love" of his is expected of almost all and everyone except himself. He alone dreads serving others and sacrificing himself for another. Human princes, military commanders and legions are thrown to their death, to acquire for him riches and glory. That is the work of Satan, the man-killer. Not so God the Lover of man, not so. He lowers Himself from the glory of the heavenly throne, to demonstrate through personal servitude and spotless sacrifice, the love of God for mankind. The love of Christ is the supreme model of courage. That is bravery, before which both death and Hell tremble.

33. Let us look now at the beginning of beginnings of human daughters. While Eve had the love of God in herself, she was entirely devoted to God. And she loved God with a divine love, with all the love in her heart, spirit and mind. The love for her husband, as well as love for all the beauties of Paradise paled before her love for God. Everything else that she loved, she loved for the sake of God and through God, but anything not seen within the radiance of her well-loved Creator, she deemed not worthy of her love. And all her soul was lightly dressed, transparent, imperceptible to the eye of the body, filled with inexpressible sweetness and delight from the love of God. In her love for the Lord God she could compete with the cherubim. Any desire whatever for someone outside of God did not enter into her heart, nor did she put her mind to it. With love towards God she lived, breathed, and rejoiced. Such was the ancestress, the mother of mankind. Such also was the first ancestor, Adam.

34. Adam and Eve had been gods, little gods, as all the heavenly angels were as well. Do not be frightened of these great words, my daughter, which are frequently repeated in holy Orthodox books. That Adam and Eve had been gods is already contained in the words of the Holy Trinity: "Let us make man in our image" (Gen. 1:26). It is recorded and the Prophet clearly stated "Ye are gods: and all of you are children of the Most High"

(Ps. 81 [82]:6). But the words are repeated for you and confirmed by the divine mouth of the Savior of the world: "Ye are gods" (Jn. 10:34). On this basis, the wise Maximus the Confessor counsels: "Let us devote ourselves to the holy Lord, that having received Him into ourselves, sanctified, through Him we may become gods." So also speak many other Orthodox theologians.

35. As long as God is seen in truth and love shining on the souls of Adam and Eve, they are really gods by any measurement the Creator has set forth for rational beings existing according to His love. That is already reinforced when Christ, in answer to the foolish question of one of the Sadducees, says that men after death "in the resurrection they neither marry, nor are given in marriage, but are as the angels of God in heaven" (Mt. 22:29-30). The angels then, are called gods by the mouth of the Psalmist: "God stands in the assembly of gods; and in the midst of them will judge gods" (Ps. 81 [82]:1).

36. Whoever was a god, even if small, did he not have freedom of action? Only the great and one eternal God, used His freedom with kindness. Satan, one of the little gods, used his freedom for evil for himself and others. So also the oldest ancestors of mankind. As soon as love was lost, their understanding darkened. With sin, freedom was also lost. If Eve had remained in the love of God, she would have borne children with her husband, "neither from bodily desire nor from lust for men, but from God."

37. In one disastrous moment, then, God-loving Eve yielded to temptation, from the corrupter of her freedom. Satan abused her, the archangel, who had become "the father of lies" (cf. Jn. 8:44), the executioner of men and the opponent of God. He whispered sweet lies into the ears of the woman. In effect, he said this to her: 'Eat of this forbidden tree, and your eyes will be opened, and you will be gods. God knows that it was for this reason forbidden you, so you will not be as He is. He cannot stand competition, He is envious.' At these words, Eve's ears buzzed, her spiritual sight was blinded, and confusion overcame her mind. She immediately confided a slander of God to the conspirator, trusting lies against the Truth, believing the murderer of man in opposition to the Lover of mankind. And in the instant when she confided in the polluted serpent with polluted lies, her soul forfeited harmony, she dismissed the chords of godly music from herself, and love turned cold for the Creator, the God of love.

38. A face does not reflect itself in troubled waters. Neither did Eve see God in the mirror of her troubled soul. She was looking at the tree, full of mixed fruit - good and bad. Looking with her confused soul, she no

longer saw God as higher than herself. She had abandoned God. God and the devil did not remain in the same regard. There was then no other woman to support her against Satan and his carnal viewpoint. And with these eyes and this new sight, she saw the forbidden fruit as good to eat, pleasant to look at and giving much knowledge. Oh, knowledge not only of good but also of evil! But the outcome of a mixture of good and evil is evil. In place of love all is filled with three desires: lust for bodily pleasure, desire for possessions, and desire for knowledge. Having lost God, she had begun to look for support in things. But the emptiness, caused by draining the abandoned God from the soul, all the world cannot fill.

39. Having separated themselves from the love of God, Adam and Eve felt fear - the eternal companion of sin - and they saw themselves as naked. As long as they were steady in their love of God, God radiated from Himself as from His temples. They were externally clothed with light, and barely regarded their own bodies. Now they were naked prior to sin, but having no consciousness of this, neither were they ashamed. But as soon as the three desires occupied the place of their love, their spiritual vision was eclipsed, and they regarded themselves with carnal eyes and saw their own bodies. Having become poor and bereft, the soul without the blessed love of God, saw only what could be seen with bodily eyes ...

40. On the tree of knowledge was a mixture of good and bad fruit. And the bad fruit was more attractive, as always, not only in taste, but in appearance, with bright colors and beautiful shapes. Deluded, curious, the woman reached out and ate first the fruit of evil and then the fruit of good. Because of this, she first gave birth to the bad Cain and then the good Abel. And from then on they continued to bear both bad and good, through all the ages and generations of men. Estrangements, conflicts, quarrels, wars filled the whole history of mankind. The history of the world is a macrocosm of the Tree of Knowledge.

41. Some have taken the sin of Eve lightly, my daughter. They say: What is so terrible about a woman having taken some forbidden fruit? They speak in this way in justification, not only of our ancestor, but also of themselves who were enticed to sin. The father of lies has called God a liar, and the woman believed him - is that not terrible? For he said to the woman: you will not die, as God has told you, but you will become gods as He is also, as soon as you eat from the forbidden tree. If he had said: you will become "gods" as I am, that would have been closer to reality. And the woman believed that God had told lies and that the devil spoke the truth. This whole process of separation from the truth of God and adherence to the father of lies, that is of the emptying of the love of God and acquisition

83

of carnal lusts; that whole process, I repeat, was originated in the soul of Eve before she grabbed the forbidden fruit. The identical process occurs today among men and women who fall into sin. The soul prepares but the flesh carries it out.

42. When men were stripped of the love of God, the one true love, they began to refer to their lusts and desires in terms of love. Such was the name for the desire for and the enjoyment of carnal delights, for earthly riches, for inquisitive knowledge, as also lust for casual union, for power, and gaining honors, for sport and feasting, for possessing things. All this men vest with the name of love according to the machinations of Satan, solely and exclusively so that heavenly love is forgotten: the one love that is not counterfeit. It was like a prisoner in darkness crumbling some black bread into small morsels, and giving these morsels the name of the most festive food which they had once eaten when they were free. It was through this lying illusion that it was possible to swallow the bitter bread of darkness.

43. A multiplicity of lusts grown out of carnal love could in no way replace real love nor make men happy. On the contrary, those who exercised them were all unhappy, for from afar they were bewitched by them and from nearby they disappointed them. In bloom it was a rose; after the bloom, it was a thornbush. Many lusts caused heartbreak, and conflicts, both internal as well as external between the sons of men. Wonderfully the apostles of God explain this. First James, the brother of the Lord: "From whence come wars and fightings among you? come they not hence, even of your lusts that war in your members? Ye lust, and have not: ye kill and desire to have, and cannot obtain ...Ye ask, and receive not, because ye ask amiss, that ye may consume it upon your lusts" (James 4:1-3). About this, Peter: "Dearly beloved, I beseech you as strangers and pilgrims, abstain from fleshly lusts, which war against the soul" (1 Peter 2:11), and Paul warns: "Walk in the Spirit, and ye shall not fulfil the lust of the flesh" (Gal. 5:16). And still many, many more that are similar.

44. Oh, my daughter, look and see how, with the loss of divine love, man's consciousness of truth was also lost. For love and truth are inseparable. Once alienated, just as many lusts replace love, so many false ideas replace truth, and false gods substitute for the one true God. All human lusts have been represented by some spurious deity. This is clearly seen from mythology, particularly the Hellenic which has worked it out to the finest detail, and regretfully, with great poetic paeans of praise. Human lusts and passions are projected onto the faces of gods and goddesses, so that men "became vain in their imaginations, and their foolish heart was

darkened. Professing themselves to be wise, they became fools" (Rom. 1:21-22).

45. They were the same three principal lusts which provoked the heart of Eve, so that her heart being emptied of love, it tasted the same evil spirits as Christ the Savior encountered in the wilderness near Jericho. These are: desire for earthly satisfaction, desire for worldly possessions that the eye sees, and desire for recognition - all outside and contrary to God and the love of God. But Jesus imperiously drives them away from Himself - not like Eve - with the words: "Get thee hence, Satan" (Mt. 4:10).

46. So said the Son of God in the beginning of His saving ministry to mankind. And at the end Jesus said to His disciples: "Behold, the prince of this world cometh" (i.e., the prince of vain lusts and lies) "and hath nothing in Me" (Jn. 14:30), that is, none of their deadly lusts. He exists between God and Satan, a distance as great as the gulf between vain lust and love.

47. Love is God. It is only through God that the created of God can love ...That is why the First Commandment intones: "Thou shalt love the Lord thy God," and then the Second: "And thou shalt love thy neighbor as thyself" (Mk. 12:30-31; cf. Deut. 6:5). Without love for God all other love is unreal and transitory. As hot weather comes and goes, giving place to frost [unaffected by man], even so, man neither by himself nor with the intellect can love without love for God. Only through God can man love himself as a creature of God. Of selflove blessed Diadochos of Photiki says: "Whoever loves himself cannot love God."

48. When Christ commanded: "Love your neighbor," He did not think as many do, that it is necessary that we love only the good and the righteous and healthy and good-looking, but also the bad and the unrighteous and sick and leprous, and the hunchbacked and the blind and crazy and unattractive and repulsive and disgusting ...

49. Love is not just one of the sentiments of the heart. Love is the queen of all noble and determinative feelings. Saint Theodore of Edessa says: "Love is truly called the mother of virtue, the primary commandment and prophet." Everything else remaining that is noble, positive, compassionate, is tantamount to her ladies in waiting. For this reason the Apostle also wrote to the Colossians that love is perfection: "Love is the bond of perfectness" (cf. Col. 3:14). But to the Thessalonians: "The Lord direct your hearts into the love of God" (2 Thess. 3:5). Truly, love is the shortest way to the kingdom of heaven. Love eliminates the distance between God and man.

50. Listen now, daughter, to this mystery. God is the perfect person; therefore He is perfect love. God is the perfect person, therefore He is also perfect truth. God is the perfect person, therefore He is also perfect life. From this Christ pronounced the words universally quoted: "I am the Way, the Truth and the Life' (Jn. 14:6), understanding by "the Way": Love. For this reason love is like a Way, put in the primary place. For it is only through love that truth and life are reached. Due to this, once more it is said in the Holy Scripture: "If any man love not the Lord Jesus Christ, let him be Anathema" (1 Cor. 16:22). If there is not an anathema, is he who is without love, then not consequently also without truth and life? From this the curse is on oneself.

51. The body can neither love nor hate. Neither can a body fall in love with a body. The capability for love belongs to the soul. When the soul is in love with the body, that is not love but desire, lust. When the soul is in love with the soul, but not through God, that is either admiration, or pity. However, when the soul, through God loves the soul, without consideration for the appearance of the body - beauty or ugliness - that is love. That is true love, my daughter. For in love is life.

52. A scholar attracts by his knowledge, a wealthy man by riches, a handsome man by beauty, an artist by his skill. Each of these attracts a limited number of individuals. Only love attracts all human beings. The attraction of love is unlimited. And educated or uneducated, rich or poor, skilled or unskilled, beautiful or ugly, healthy or sick, and young or old - all want to be loved. Christ spread His love on everyone, and lovingly drew all to Himself. With His great love he encompassed even the dead, long decomposed and forgotten by men.

53. Mankind, even the dead, desire to be loved. And even after death they struggle with death. Therefore much effort is made with testaments and memorials to assure themselves of love even after death. And living and dead, men desire to be loved. Certainly relatives can have the love of their kin, though dying as paupers. But Christ said "And I, if I be lifted up from the earth, will draw all men unto Me" (Jn. 12:32). Lifted up on the cross, He has drawn through His life, out of love, all towards Himself, even the souls of the deceased from Hell. Before Christ, my daughter, there did not exist a science of love, nor a religion of love.

EPILOGUE I: LESSONS IN DIVINE AND CHRISTIAN LOVE

54. The beloved apostle and epistle writer, St. John, wrote: "Love not the world, neither the things that are in the world. If any man love the world, the love of the Father is not in him" (1 Jn. 2:15). And he gave the reason why one should not love the world, because: "all that is in the world, the lust of the flesh, the lust of the eyes, and the pride of life, is not of the Father, but is of the world. And the world passeth away, and the lust thereof: but he that doeth the will of God abideth for ever" (1 Jn. 2:16-17). These three, then: the lust of the flesh, the lust of the eyes, and the pride of life (particularly for recognition) - are three ancient evils, with which Satan deceived Eve, but not Christ as well.

55. St. Antony the Great said: "The beginning of sin was lust; the beginning of salvation and the kingdom of heaven was love." Love and lust are opposites. Whoever calls lust by the name of love, sins against love. For love is spiritual, pure and holy, but lust is carnal, impure and profane. Love is inseparable from truth, and lust is inseparable from delusion and lies. It is natural for real love to grow continuously in strength and ardor without consideration of human age; lust on the other hand, quickly passes, transforming itself into loathing, and frequently leading to despondence.

56. That which among the beasts is not for condemnation, is to be condemned among men. All our knowledge of animals cannot explicate the interior feeling of animals. We do not know what is inside them, but only what is on the surface. Still we can say for certain that they live according to their nature by the grace and predetermination of the creator. From their origin, they live in the same way, each according to its gender and unerring. It is not possible to speak of sin among animals. But man commits sin if he lives in accordance with beastial lusts. And still such lusts are called by the holy name of love! Neither can man lower himself to the level of an animal without lowering himself even below the animal.

57. If someone says: but man also has to live according to his nature, we ask by whose nature? Is that according to his fundamental, innocent, paradisial nature, as God created man, or according to his other diseased, degraded, demonic, polluted, sinful, disfigured, passionate, benumbed nature? For God did not create men as He created all the rest of nature, but in a special manner. Moreover, He gave them all power over and above the rest of nature. In this man is clearly exceptional to other physical natures: fish, birds, beasts, and raised above all the animal kingdom, even monkeys or apes. Christ came to restore this first and true human nature. And only one who lives according to this restored nature lives truly in accordance with the nature of humankind. Zoology lies under the feet of anthropology.

58. Man restored through Christ lives with a restored nature, and a restored mind, heart and will. All these three "measures" of the soul are raised in him by the leaven of the Holy Spirit (cf. Mt. 13:33). Ultimately these three components contain within themselves the trinitarian heavenly love, which "passeth understanding" [cf. Phil 4:7]. Therefore the Apostle speaks of a "new man" in the likeness of Christ, and in the same way the great Apostle: "Old things are passed away; behold things are become new" (2 Cor. 5:17).

59. As the old passes away, and the new comes into being; as rusted iron turns to brilliant steel; as a hill layered with dirt collapses into the abyss, these burdens weigh on the shoulders of humanity. For this, a power greater than man is necessitated for all creatures, even those who despise themselves. On earth, such a force does not exist, neither such love, nor such heroism. This needed to come from heaven. And it has come. For "God so loved the world, that He gave His only begotten Son, that whoever believed in Him should not perish, but have everlasting life" (Jn. 3:16). Therefore the Son of God came down from heaven, "the power of God and the wisdom of God" to revive by His love the world that was dead.

60. On two occasions, the love of Christ touched the earth: first when He died by suffering on the cross to redeem mankind from sin and death, and the second time when He rose in radiance and in glory, releasing those who had been imprisoned in Hades. These two seismic events happened and are past. But the upheaval in the heart of man caused by His burning love continues, having started with the troop of His apostles and the myrrh-bearing women, extending through the army of His numerous disciples who followed, and through all the ages and over the surface of all the earth. Inflamed with the fire of the love of Christ, His erstwhile pursuer shouted: "I count all but dung, that I may win Christ" (Phil. 3:8).

61. This same Saul - Paul - writes like lightning and not with a feather: "Who shall separate us from the love of God? shall tribulation or distress, or persecution, or famine, or nakedness, or peril, or sword? As it is written, For Thy sake we are killed all the day long; we are accounted as sheep for the slaughter. Nay, in all these things we are more than conquerers through Him that loved us. For I am persuaded that neither death, nor life, nor angels, nor principalities, nor powers, nor things present nor things to come, nor height, nor depth, nor any other creature, shall be able to separate us from the love of God, which is in Christ Jesus our Lord" (Rom. 8:35-39). Know, my daughter, that all the infernal swarm retreats before a man with such love.

EPILOGUE I: LESSONS IN DIVINE AND CHRISTIAN LOVE

62. "I am come to send fire on the earth" (Lk. 12:49) said the Lord. That is the heavenly fire of love, from which is no smoke, nor anything carnal or material, nor lustful nor unholy. This kind of love elated all the apostles, as also many saints and saintly. Their hearts were emptied of carnal and transient lusts, and they lifted themselves up solely to Him, to the one Beloved, not seeking anything worldly and having given up everything of the world for His sake.

63. Such sainted love could be carried only in a person, but not in any principle or law or nature. Look, even earthly love - such as one can give the name of love - is tied to some person, and not to a principle, or law, or some inarticulate creation. In vain have earthly wisdoms struggled, both before and after Christ, to persuade the people of an impersonal God. It was like water poured into a sieve. Yet even the people who have believed in a personal God, or gods, in no way whatever in their pantheons have they had one God with such and so much love, who revealed Himself to the world in actuality through the person of Jesus Christ, the God-Man.

64. The love which Christ has shown the world, my daughter, was love "before the foundation of the world" (Jn. 17:24). Such love then is timeless and ageless; it is not exterior, but interior. "I am in My Father, and ye in Me, and I in you" (Jn. 14:20). Where the Son is there is the Father and the Holy Spirit. He desires for His love to fill the trinitarian existence of the human soul. Although He is the head of the household, nevertheless He knocks as a humble guest at the door of every heart of man. For free will has been given to man, and He does not force Himself on man. Blessed is he who subjugates his freedom to His love. "I will come in to him, and will sup with him, and he with Me" (Rev. 3:20). Happy is he who voluntarily opens his heart to Jesus who offers His love, and with this love also life and peace and joy.

65. Out of love for the soul of man the Lord Christ worries also about the body of man as a vehicle for the soul. He nourishes the hungry in the deserts, gives treatment to the people with bodily ills, saves them from storm and weather, cleanses them from evil spirits. He touches the festering eyes of the blind, puts His hand on the leprous and the dead, straightens the crippled and hunchbacked. And the hunchbacked, my daughter, he does not forget. The most repulsive body is not turned away by Him, any more than the most beautiful and attractive. He counts Himself one with souls who develop and mature in their bodily vessels. Everybody with spiritual fruit he counts. And He already knows, that frequently the most hunchbacked appletree gives the sweetest fruit. Remember that, daughter.

66. God knows the value of men's bodies. What is the body? He has said it through His prophets and apostles and priestly poets: a puff of smoke that vanishes, an herb that withers, a flower that wilts, dust from dust. Men look at the cart from shortsightedness and vanity; they look at the vehicle but not at the coachman. He, however, first looks at the coachman hidden in the vehicle. All His concern and love are directed towards the invisible coachman, that is for the soul within the body. But when He has repaired and cleaned the wagon, He has done it for the coachman. If He heals and builds up the human body, it is because of the immortal human soul. For "what is man profited, if he shall gain the whole world, and lose his own soul?" (Mt. 16:20).

67. The Lord Jesus has repeated again and again the reminder to men, that they should not worry about food and drink and clothing. Those are the main cares of the pagans but not of His followers. It is not worthy of the sons of God, that those concerns which are uppermost in animals should also be the main concerns of men. The one who has called us as His guests in this world knows our needs and attends to them for us. Or do we think that God is a poorer householder than a human householder? God forbid. Despite all our worries for the body we cannot be saved from old age, sickness, death and decay. Nevertheless we know that the Almighty has clothed our souls in this mysteriously woven tapestry, this body, fashioned from earthly materials. We consider it precious but Him we deem secondary, who will clothe us after death in an incomparably beautiful body, immortal and incorruptible, which will not suffer nor age. That is promised to us by the One who created us out of pure love, and who reserves His love as response to our love.

68. Love for God expels all fear from the soul except fear of sin. Yes, love reinforces fear of sin: fear of sin that is also fear of God. The great lovers of Christ were not afraid either of men or beasts or poverty or death. They even rejoiced in suffering for Him, who had suffered for them, seeking only to become like Him. They desired to die and leave this world without delay, so as to be with their beloved Lord as soon as possible. The Apostle testified to this: "We are confident ...and willing rather to be absent from the body, and to be present with the Lord" (2 Cor. 5:8). "For we know that if our earthly house of this tabernacle were dissolved, we have ...an house ...eternal in the heavens." Then he says: "For this we groan, earnestly desiring to be clothed upon with our house which is in heaven" (2 Cor. 5:1-2).

69. Christ recommends to those who follow Him, not some earthly model of love, but divine love: "If ye keep My commandments, ye shall abide in My love; even as I have kept My Father's commandments, and

abide in His love" (Jn. 15:10). And all His commandments are contained in one: "Love." All His other commandments, such as: the command to prayer, to give alms, humility, purity, forbearance, self-sacrifice, bravery, carefreeness, forgiveness, vigilance, joy are simply rays emanating from His love. He who obtains the queen of virtues, also obtains her royal retinue.

70. In all the books of the New Testament love is placed above all other virtues and commandments, since it encompasses all. Recognized everywhere are the words of the Apostle Paul about love: "Though I speak with the tongues of men and of angels, and have not love, I am become as sounding brass, or a tinkling cymbal. And though I have the gift of prophecy, and understand all mysteries, and all knowledge, and though I have all faith, so that I could remove mountains, and have not love, I am nothing. And though I bestow all my goods to feed the poor, and though I give my body to be burned, and have not love, it profiteth me nothing. Love suffereth long, and is kind; love envieth not; love vaunteth not itself, is not puffed up, Doth not behave itself unseemly, seeketh not her own, is not easily provoked, thinketh no evil; Rejoiceth not in iniquity, but rejoiceth in the truth; Beareth all things, believeth all things, hopeth all things, endureth all things. Love never faileth: but whether there be prophecies, they shall fail; whether there be tongues, they shall cease; whether there be knowledge, it shall vanish away. For we know in part, and we prophesy in part. But when that which is perfect is come, then that which is in part shall be done away. When I was a child, I spake as a child, I understood as a child, I thought as a child: but when I became a man, I put away childish things. For now we see through a glass darkly; but then face to face: now I know in part; but then shall I know even as also I am known. And now abideth faith, hope, love, these three; but the greatest of these is love" (1 Cor. 13: 1-13). Never was uttered anything so beautiful by hymn or by the tongue of men.

71. When divine love came to the heart of man, with it came everything - all - my daughter: wisdom and power and purity and compassion and righteousness and bravery and endurance and clairvoyance and tranquillity and joy and every goodness. But that is completely logical. For God "that spared not His own Son, but delivered Him up for us all, how shall He not with Him also freely give us all things?" (Rom. 8:32). The entire history of the Church confirms this. By the illuminations of the love of Christ, bumpkins have developed wisdom, cowards become martyrs, rakes saints, misers benefactors, kings and rich men slaves of Christ, wolves lambs, and lambs lions. The wondrous strength of Christ's love has not ceased with His departure but has still multiplied, very much increased.

72. Christ has given all His love to men. This is why He expects all their love on the part of men. And from you too, my dear soul. Not only did He proscribe the division of our heart between God and Mammon, but He demanded something that appeared completely against man's nature. "He that loveth father or mother more than Me is not worthy of Me: and he that loveth son or daughter more than Me is not worthy of Me" (Mt. 10:37), then in reinforcement: "If any man ...hate not his father, and mother, and wife, and children, and brethren, and sisters, yea, and his own life also, he cannot be My disciple" (Lk. 14:26). Naturally, that is impossible for all men except those who open their hearts to God. Then the Almighty makes the impossible possible. "Love naturally has nothing except God, for God is love," wrote St. Nilus of Sinai.

73. As long as man does not feel hatred for his old robe, he does not wish for a new one. How could the words "a new creature in Christ," "new man," "sons of light," have come into being if we had not felt hatred for our old sinful soul, which through enslavement to the body had developed a carnal rather than a spiritual existence. An old man is entirely in fear of God. Fear is for us the beginning and the end. In the new man, fear is the beginning, love is the end. Death for the love of Christ is a guarantee of life eternal.

74. Whoever estranges himself from the love of Christ, falls into the foolishness of bodily lusts which do not know moderation and are number-less. In those who are illuminated by love, carnal lusts do not rule; they are indifferent toward the delusions of this temporal world. They "use this world, as not abusing it: for the fashion of this world passeth away" (1 Cor. 7:31). They see the things invisible and not those that are visible. Their attention is continually directed to the tomb, towards Him whom they love and who has prepared for them: "Eye hath not seen, nor ear heard, neither have entered into the heart of man, the things which God hath prepared for them that love Him" (cf. 1 Cor. 2:9). That is the final goal of our journey and of our efforts. Our shorter perspectives are illusory.

75. Man cannot have true and constant love towards God without first acquiring love for Christ. Neither can he have love for his neighbor without first having love for Christ. This we repeat and will repeat. As it has been said: "In the light we become light." Therefore it can be said: through love of You we also love. For only through love of God, incarnated in Christ, can we truly love both God and ourselves and our neighbor, and even our enemies. Because Christ died also for our enemies. Exclusively through this great price, by which Christ redeemed our enemies, to love them has been made possible for us, and to bless and pray for them. All this is

through Christ, and not through our enemies. Saint Maximus the Confessor writes: "Whoever loves God will inevitably love his neighbor." We add: Whoever is unable to love God, does not love Christ the incarnate Son of God. In the New Testament two basic dogmas are revealed to the world: the Holy Trinity and the Incarnate Son of God. Love rests on those two dogmas.

76. God has blessed marriage: first in Paradise, afterwards also in Cana. In marriage, two bodies become one flesh; two souls "inseparable and without confusion," two temples of the Holy Spirit under one roof. Why does God unite two bodies in one? Because, "it is easier for a pair on the road than one." For in marriage, impure lusts of the body are bridled: the irrational by purpose. For it enables multiplication of the human species and multiplies those who preserve the sacrifice of Christ. Moreover, bodily nuptials of man and wife, linked in love, and blessed by the Church, are the most expressive symbol of Christ's spiritual union with the Church and with each Christian spirit. And among the first followers of the Lord, the apostles and the myrrhbearers, were also both the married and the unmarried.

77. Monasticism is in concept supernatural, angelic. In innumerable examples, monastics have proved themselves and demonstrated themselves in practice to be supernatural and angelic. But according to the words of our Lord Himself: "All men cannot receive this saying, save they to whom it is given" (Mt. 19:11). It is given to those in whom the vision of the heavenly kingdom has clearly been opened; whose hearts have been opened exclusively to the love of Christ; those who have lifted themselves gladly up steep spiritual cliffs to the altitude of heaven, and who have felt the call of grace and the power of God ... In this way Christ encourages the monastic life: "He that is able to receive it, let him receive it" (Mt. 19:12). Blessed are you, my daughter, for you yourself have been able to receive that which all cannot receive, for you have chosen the love that is not divided.

78. The Apostle Paul, an unmarried apostle, and with the mind of a celibate, highlights such service in the name of the Lord, saying (but not commanding): "I would that all men were even as myself." And he repeated: "to the unmarried and widows: it is good for them if they abide even as I" (1 Cor. 7- 8). And in many ways the apostle commends celibacy for the sake of the Lord, as much as he condemns the celibate for carnal desires. In the first case love for the Lord replaces all carnal lust, in the second, desires and lusts drive out love and exchange places with them.

79. Monasticism is not created, but is an exception, yet an exception without which the Church of Christ would not have been nor will be in existence. It resembles those irregular verbs (like the verb "to be"), without which speech is incomplete.

80. The great austerity of monastic life in the Orthodox Church is possible only for those who endure, those who have great love for the Lord. Because of it, they have become "the light of the world" and "earthly angels and heavenly men," a model of prayer and fasting, right faith and purity. "Whoever loves to converse with Christ, loves solitude," according to the great St. Isaac the Syrian. A conversation of love with love in solitude.

81. In the Lives of the Saints we find extraordinary examples, where a married couple, by mutual agreement, continued to live a chaste life as brother and sister (Galaction and Epistima, Alexis the Man of God, etc.), according to the preaching of the Apostle Paul: "that both they that have wives be as though they had none" (1 Cor. 7:29). The conquerors of carnal lust were victorious over the serpent which overcame Eve in Paradise.

82. The New Testament speaks sufficiently and clearly of married life. The holy Apostle, with fatherly love and severity, has counselled husbands and wives and children as well. The mastery of the husband over the wife is compared with Christ's role as the head of the Church (1 Pet. 3:1-8). The love of the husband for the wife is expected to be similar to the love of Christ towards the Church (1 Tim. 2:9-15; 5:1-15), for which He gave Himself as a sacrifice (1 Cor. 7:1-16). The married wife is saved in the birth of children, if she continues in the faith and with love, holiness, and honor (cf. 1 Cor. 7:14). But she who lives in fleshly pleasures, is dead while she lives. Children should respect and obey their parents. There is no kinship without obligation.

83. A consecrated marriage symbolizes the unity of Christ with His holy Church, and in Christ a spiritual union with the spirit of all the faithful. Inversely, infidelity and debauchery symbolize satanism, betrayal of the love of God, severance of one's union with God. But that is in effect exactly the thing Satan desires: to frustrate and make a travesty of the love of God in men. Pure heavenly love is odious to Satan, but he relishes carnal lust and all impurity: the "unfruitful works of darkness" (Eph. 5:11). Those are his lures with which he decoys men to the inferno.

84. In the Holy Scripture of God, adultery and debauchery are frequently called apostasy from the one God, and the worship of idols. The prophets and apostles have thunderously condemned both those shameful

sins as leprosy of the soul. Whether a man has been unfaithful to his wife, or whether he has worshipped idols, in both events he apostasizes from God and satisfies the desire of Satan. Love has nothing in common with adultery or debauchery, which only simulate love.

85. There is yet another offense against love that is as grave as debauchery and adultery - even more grave. That is to be a contestant of God as a hypocritical leader of the people: one who declares his love for the people with the tongue, but in his soul scorns the people. Under cover of the law he cheats and oppresses the people, while abandoning "truth, mercy and faith." For these hypocrites, God is an impediment and Christ an annoyance, and with their guile they devise ways to estrange and crucify Christ. These are the greatest enemies of the people, who persecute and kill the true friends of the people. One of them Christ placed below a harlot and a publican, saying to the Pharisee: "Verily I say unto you, that the publicans and the harlots go into the kingdom before you" (Mt. 21:31).

86. The fragrance of love! When we burn incense, we think of the fragrant heavenly aroma of love. The Holy Spirit, like a heavenly fire, brings the warmth of love into the human heart, and like a fresh wind, chases away the stench of sin and spreads the aroma of Christ to the world. That savor all the saints have borne within themselves. People have sensed it in living saints and in their relics. The Apostle speaks of this: "We are unto God a sweet savour of Christ," the sweet perfume of recognition of the truth and the sweetness of love (cf. 2 Cor. 2:14-16).

87. The hymns of the Church chant of the "fragrant Paradise." That aroma, emanating from the Lord, flows through the Lord and all His followers to all in whom the stench of human lust has been replaced by the blessed perfume of the love of God. But the aroma of Christ did not affect all in the same way, for "to one we are the savour of death unto death; and to the other the savour of life unto life" (2 Cor. 2:16). For some dissipate the aroma of Christ with the stench of sin, while others preserve it to the end, guarding their hearts and laboring with love, that in all things they should be pleasing to Christ, and receive within themselves "the fragrance of Paradise."

88. "I have espoused you to one husband, that I may present you as a chaste virgin to Christ" (2 Cor. 11:2), wrote Paul to the Corinthians, who were sunk in carnal lusts and infamy. That is the mission of the Church: namely to purify the faithful from all corruption, sins and passions, and to render their souls pure and holy like the virgins, the brides of the most chaste and holy Christ the King. St. Theognostus writes: "There is no other

such great ascesis as that of chastity and virginity. Those who honorably maintain the state of chastity, provoke the admiration of angels and obtain the wreath of the martyr." The popular Serbian folk epic chants of "the savor of the virginal soul." That is the savor of purity and holiness, my daughter.

89. In the East the people are aware of distinctions between the aroma of a baptized and an unbaptized soul. Bees, by odor, sense men as enemies and immediately attack. Wild beasts approaching holy men and women, ingratiate themselves to them. The savor of love is sensed. Mark how the apostles sensed that unearthly odor of love (cf. Phil. 4:18). God cannot abide incense oblations from strange, lawless people and from vain hypocrites (cf. Isa. 1:13) ...

90. Love forgives much. And through love everything is pardoned. Proud justification of oneself is contrary to love. The Pharisee Simon wanted to mock Jesus for allowing a woman who was an obvious sinner to wash His feet with her repentant tears and to wipe them with her hair (recognizing that she had sins as many as hairs on her head). Jesus reprimanded the Pharisee, saying: "Her sins, which are many, are forgiven, for she loved much" (Lk. 7:47). For whom was the love? For Him, who was on the road to Golgotha and because her sins and those of the whole world were to be wiped away not by tears but by His blood.

91. Christ, out of love, sought us - but not ours. But men, because of their meager love, seek His good things rather than Him. They expect from Him bread, rain, fertility, health, and earthly goods in general. And He gives all with sadness that it is not Him, Himself they seek. They have forgotten that when they have received Him, they have received all along with Him. The Apostle said: "I do count them all as dung, that I may win Christ" (Phil 3:8). Elsewhere he writes to the faithful: "I seek not yours but you" (2 Cor. 12:14).

92. Love and a dowry are not compatible. You have bitter experience of this personally, my daughter. Where there is a demand for a dowry, there is an absence of love. In the *Troparion* of the holy virginal martyrs of the Orthodox hymnology their love for Christ is wonderfully described: "O Jesus, your lamb [*Name*] cries out to You with great love: 'O my Bridegroom, I long for You in great pain ... I die for You in order to live in You. Accept me as an immaculate victim, since I am immolated for Your love.'" That is what Christ expects of His brides: their soul, with flaming love, and not their dowry. Your three fiances, my daughter, had no intention of giving themselves to you, but only to sell themselves.

93. Christ as bridegroom and His mystical marriage with individual souls and with the Church universal has been the subject of much Orthodox theology. In the parable of the nuptials of the Royal Son, it is obvious that Christ is presenting Himself as the Royal Son and Bridegroom. But His reference to nuptials rather than marriage indicates that He expects a union in marriage with many human souls, who in this life love Him as He loves them. Not all who are invited respond to the call, for there are many bound to carnal lusts and wedded to the world. But even without them, "the wedding was furnished with guests" (Mt. 22:10). In this way, too, the heavenly kingdom, the nuptial chamber of Christ, would fill itself with the souls of the faithful and with those who would love Him. But whoever was missing, was absent not because he had not received a call, but because, according to his will he did not desire to be invited to the call.

94. But whatever is likely to be our human destiny on earth; what kinds of intrigues and obstacles come from Satan and from pagans, and however many there will yet be in the last times that apostate from the truth and the love of Christ, still the kingdom of Christ will undoubtedly be filled. Or would He, who has taught us that when we want to build walls to the tower we must first calculate whether we can finish, would He in advance not have calculated how the kingdom is to be filled? The Church is His body. What kind of body would it be without all its members, even to the tiniest cell? Therefore the Lord will purge and revive many repentant sinners - male and female - so that they may worthily call themselves His brides. But only with repentance a beginning is made of the personal struggle for the encounter with the grace of God.

95. Just as parents rejoice when someone loves or honors their children, so also the Lord is glad when men love and glorify His saints. For it is the same as glorifying God. "Whoever receives you receives Me," (Mt. 10:40), He said. And whoever glorifies the saints of Christ, Christ glorifies. The saints celebrated their Lord on earth with divine love, and in the face of all temptation kept His commandments. So they overcame the ancient monster of malevolence and malice, the first mankiller. And not seeking anything for themselves on earth, they receive everything in heaven. Thus has also been promised, (not by the lying lips of man but by the veritable mouth of God): "He that overcometh shall inherit all things; and I will be his God, and he shall be My son" (Rev. 21:7).

96. Who will overcome? Those who know that they are part of the body of Christ, and those who hold their body and soul to be sacred, not as if it were their own but as belonging to Christ: they will be victors. Those who look at Christ crucified on the cross and then say to themselves: there

is the One who loves me more than my mother; His sufferings are for my sins, and His blood for my purification and salvation: they will overcome. All those will be victors who through time have adorned their soul with trembling love for Christ, the eternal Bridegroom. Yes, all those who respond to the call to the heavenly supper with the Lamb of God. "Blessed are they which are called unto the marriage supper of the Lamb" (Rev. 19:9). Called and responded. Fear of the Lord is the beginning of wisdom; love is the fulness and the culmination of wisdom.

97. All men are called and God desires that all respond. And indeed many, very many have responded in the course of past ages and still many will respond. That will be such a great gathering as if the sands had come to human life. That assembly the Mystagogue John the Divine described thus: "After this I beheld, and, lo, a great multitude, which no man could number, of all nations, and kindreds, and people, and tongues, stood before the throne, and before the Lamb, clothed with white robes, and palms in their hands" (Rev. 7:9). Such a celebration, such joy, is neither known nor accessible on earth. That is a celebration of love, which truly exceeds all understanding and every imagination. That is the immeasurable, immense kingdom of Christ.

98. Watch, my daughter, and do not deceive yourself. How tender the love of the Lamb for those who with fear and love answer the call of the Father to the marriage of the Son. And how terrible the anger of the Lamb against those who have received the call but have not responded; if they should reject it or tear it up or call apostles, missionaries, priests to suffer martyrdom. For when the Lamb of God overcomes all the monsters in human or non-human form, and reveals himself to the world, then those will scream in terror "to the mountains and the rocks, Fall on us, and hide us from the face of Him that sitteth on the throne and from the wrath of the Lamb" (Rev. 6:16). But just and dreadful will be the retribution for love betrayed.

99. When one of the spouses is unfaithful to the spousal fidelity, how much anger, how much hatred, how much noise! In the meantime, neither of the spouses has sacrificed beforehand for their marital partner, not one eye, not one hand, not one finger. Nevertheless, so much passion! But Christ gave all of His body for us as a sacrifice, all His blood to pour out for all the souls of men ...

100. Love does not need the law. Love is a law above laws. It is the New Law, or the New Testament of Christ. "We know that all things work together for good for them that love God" (Rom. 8:28). The road of love

can be full of obstacles and difficulties, but according to the word of God and the experience of men, that road leads unerringly in the direction of the greatest good.

101. I have written much to you, daughter of God, and all of it can be briefly summed up like this: "If you love the Lord Jesus Christ, you have already fulfilled both of the great commandments of love. For He is God, and He is your neighbor. Yes, our closest neighbor. The two commandments of love personally relate to Him: and in the first place to Him. In older times, men were unable to love an invisible God. Jesus Christ is both God manifest and authenticated Man. The God-Man, who as God showed Himself as the God of love, as Man immolated Himself for us as the Man of Love. Truly I say to you, for that kind of God and that kind of neighbor, to love is absolutely easy, and through Him to love all that are His.

102. O my soul, Kassiana, hasten to foresake all, and let all abandon you. Friends will forget you. Wealth will be without profit for you; beauty will fade, vigor will vanish, the body will decompose, and the soul will otherwise find itself in gloom. Who will stretch out hands to you in the darkness and isolation? One: Christ, the Lover of Mankind, provided that you have been united with Him during your life. He will lead you out of the darkness to the light, and from isolation to the Heavenly Assembly. Think of this instruction day and night and direct your soul in accordance with it. Let Christ the Lord, the King of Love, come to your aid. Amen.

Note: This writing I consecrate to my spiritual daughter, the nun Kassiana, for perusal and meditation and to Him who is the greatest in heaven and on earth.

The humble servant of God,
+ Callistratus.

EPILOGUE - PART II

THE SONG OF EVE AND HER DESCENDANTS

1. Moses sang: (Ex. 15:1, 2, 6, 13, 16, 17, 18, LXX).

Let us sing to the Lord, for He is very greatly glorified ...He was to me a helper and protector for salvation; this is my God, and I will glorify Him...

Your right hand, O God, has been glorified in strength; Your right hand, O God, has broken the enemies...

You have guided in Your righteousness this Your people whom You have redeemed; by Your strength You have called them into Your holy resting-place...

Let trembling and fear fall upon [the nations] ...till Your people pass over, O Lord...

Bring them in and plant them in the mountain of their inheritance, in Your prepared habitation, which You, O Lord, have prepared: the sanctuary, O Lord, which Your hands have made ready. The Lord reigns for ever and ever and ever.

And Eve sang:

Let those, O Savior, who have tempted and deceived us be cast into the deep, and let Christ our Redeemer, My Lord and my God, reach out His hand to us who weep and trust in Him.

2. And Moses sang: (Deut. 32: 3, 4, 5, 6, 7, 18, 19, 20, 28, 37, 39, 40, cf. 43).

I have called on the name of the Lord; render majesty to our God. As for God, His works are true, and all His ways are judgment; God is faithful, and there is no unrighteousness in Him; just and holy is the Lord.

They have sinned, not pleasing Him, spotted children, a crooked and perverse generation. Do you thus recompense the Lord? Is the people so foolish and unwise? Did not He Himself your father purchase you, and make you and form you? Remember the days of old, consider the years for past ages...

You have forsaken God who begot you, and forgotten God who feeds you. And the Lord saw, and was jealous, and was provoked by the anger of His sons and daughters, and said, I will turn away My face from them...

It is a nation that has lost counsel, neither is there understanding in them...

And the Lord said ...Behold, behold that I AM, and there is no god beside Me; I kill, and I will make to live; I will smite, and I will heal, and there is none who shall deliver out of My hands ...I live for ever.

And Eve sang:

The Lord shall purify the land of His people. May Christ our Redeemer purify our dry bones as they lie in the valley and bring them to new and eternal life.

3. And Hannah sang: (I Kings [Samuel] 2:1, 2, 3, 6, 8, 9).

My heart is established in the Lord ...I have rejoiced in my salvation.

For there is none holy as the Lord, and there is none righteous as our God, and there is none holy beside You...

For the Lord is a God of knowledge and God prepares His own designs... The Lord kills and makes alive; he brings down to the grave, and brings up... He lifts up the poor from the earth, and raises the needy from the dunghill; to seat him with the princes of the people, and causing them to inherit the throne of glory.

He grants his petition to him that prays; and He blesses the years of the righteous, for by strength cannot man prevail.

THE LAMENT OF EVE

And Eve sang:

He has granted me children by His great benevolence and given me favor in the midst of my perdition.

4. And Habbakuk, the Prophet, sang: (Hab. 3:2, 3, 4, 13, 16, 17, 18).

O Lord, I have heard Your report, and I was afraid; I was amazed: You will be known between the two living creatures, You will be acknowledged when the years draw near.

You will be manifested when the time is come; when my soul is troubled, You will in wrath remember mercy.

God shall come from Thaeman, and the Holy One from the dark shady mount Pharan. His excellence covered the heavens, and the earth was full of His praise...

You went forth for the salvation of Your people, to save Your anointed...

I watched, and my belly trembled at the sound of the prayer on my lips, and trembling entered into my bones, and my frame was troubled within me ...Though the fig tree shall bear no fruit, and there shall be no produce on the vines ...Yet I will exult in the Lord, I will joy in God my Savior.

And Eve sang:

For He has looked down on us in our distress. He has sent His Son, His Holy One, His anointed, to bring us salvation.

5. And Isaiah, the Prophet, sang: (Isa. 26: 9, 10, 12, 13, 16, 17, 18, 19).

My spirit seeks You very early in the morning, O God, for Your commandments are a light on the earth; learn righteousness, you that dwell upon the earth. For the ungodly one is put down; no one who will not learn righteousness on the earth shall be able to execute truth. Let the ungodly be taken away, that he see not the glory of the Lord...

O Lord our God, give us peace: for You have rendered to us all things. O Lord our God, take possession of us. O Lord, we know not any other beside You; we name Your name...

Lord, in affliction I remembered You; Your chastening was to us a small affliction.

And as a woman in travail draws near to be delivered, and cries out in her pain, so have we been to Your Beloved. We have conceived, O Lord, because of fear of You, and have been in pain, and have brought forth the spirit of Your salvation, which we have wrought upon the earth...

The dead shall rise, and they that are in the tombs shall be raised, and they that are in the earth shall rejoice; for the dew from You is healing to them, but the land of the ungodly shall perish.

And Eve sang:

Be warned, all my children, and be lifted up. For Christ the Redeemer has visited this earth. He has given hope of life to the godly, but He will judge the ungodly in His Coming.

6. And Jonah, the Prophet, sang: (Jonah 2:3-10).

I cried in my affliction to the Lord my God, and he hearkened to me; even to my cry out of the belly of hell You heard my voice...

And I said, I am cast out of Your presence; shall I indeed look again towards Your holy temple?

Water has poured around me to the soul ...I went down into the earth, whose bars are the everlasting barriers; yet O Lord my God, let my ruined life be restored.

When my soul was failing me, I remembered the Lord; and may my prayer come to You in Your holy temple.

Those who observe vanities and lies have forsaken their own mercy. But I will sacrifice to You with the voice of praise and thanksgiving; all that I have vowed I will pay to You, the Lord of my salvation.

And Eve sang:

Let us praise Christ, our Lord God and Savior who lifts us out of our tombs of death and corruption.

And the Church sang: (*Service Book*, Isabel Hapgood, p. 446 - from Orthodox Requiem for the Dead).

Ikos: You only are immortal, who have created and fashioned man. For out of the earth were we mortals made, and unto the earth shall we return again, as You did command when You made me, saying unto me: For earth You are, and unto the earth shall You return. Whither also all we mortals wend our way, making of our funeral dirge the song: Alleluia.

7.   And the Three Holy Children sang: (Daniel 3-Apocrypha vs. 2-13, 15-17).

Blessed are You, O Lord God of our fathers: Your name is worthy to be praised and glorified for ever more. For You are righteous in all the things that You have done to us; yes true are all Your works, Your ways are right, and all Your judgments are truth.

In all the things that you have brought upon us ...You brought all these things upon us because of our sins. For we have sinned and committed iniquity, departing from You. In all things have we trespassed, and not obeyed Your commandments...

And You delivered us into the hands of lawless enemies, most hateful forsakers of God ...And now we cannot open our mouths, we are become a shame and reproach to Your servants, and to those that worship You.

Yet deliver us not up wholly, for Your name's sake ...and cause not Your mercy to depart from us ...For we, O Lord, are become less than any nation...

Nevertheless in a contrite heart and in humble spirit let us be accepted. Like as in the burnt offerings of rams and bullocks ...so let our sacrifice be in Your sight this day, and grant that we may wholly go after You; for they shall not be confounded that put their trust in You. And now we follow You with all our heart, we fear You, and seek Your face.

And Eve sang:

Out of the dust into which my soul has sunk, hear my prayer of contrition, supplication, thanksgiving and praise, O Lord, who are bountiful and full of compassion.

8. And the Three Holy Children sang: (Daniel - Apocrypha vs. 28-32, 34, 36, 51, 59).

Blessed are You, O Lord God of our fathers, and to be praised and exalted above all for ever. And blessed is Your glorious and holy name, and to be praised and exalted above all for ever.

Blessed are You in the temple of Your holy glory, and to be praised and glorified above all for ever. Blessed are You who behold the depths, and sits upon the cherubim, and to be praised and exalted above all for ever. Blessed are You on the glorious throne of Your kingdom, and to be praised and glorified above all for ever...

O all you works of the Lord, bless the Lord, praise and exalt Him above all for ever ...All you angels of the Lord, bless the Lord, praise and exalt Him above all for ever...

O let the earth bless the Lord, praise and exalt Him above all for ever...

O you children of men, bless the Lord, praise and exalt Him above all for ever.

And Eve sang:

Let Your majesty, wisdom, power, dominion and primacy be always and ever in our minds, O Lord God of mercy, that we may behold Your face and Your glory unto all eternity, and be transformed into Your likeness.

9. And Mary, the Mother of God, sang: (Lk. 1:46-51).

My soul magnifies the Lord, and my spirit has rejoiced in God my Savior. For He has regarded the lowly state of His maidservant; for behold, henceforth all generations will call me blessed.

For He who is mighty has done great things for me, and holy is His name. And His mercy is on those who fear Him from generation to generation.

He has shown strength with His arm; He has scattered the proud in the imagination of their hearts.

And Eve sang:

My heart leaps with pride and triumphant joy in beholding Mary, my long hoped-for daughter: how by her meekness, love, purity, and obedience she reversed my great sins of pride, apostasy, adultery, and disobedience.

By the virginity and kenosis - willing sacrifice - of her spirit, soul and body, God deemed her meet to bear our Savior : He who by His death on the tree of the cross reversed the sin Adam and I committed through the tree.

My soul will forever praise her example: a handmaiden of God, a helpmate for mankind to all eternity, subservient with joy to the will of her Master.

And the Church sang: (Paschal *Troparion*)

Christ is risen from the dead, trampling down death by death, and upon those in the tombs bestowing life.

EPILOGUE - PART III

PSALM 118 [1]

THE WAY, THE TRUTH AND THE LIFE

How can we have true life by living according to God's will? How can we restore ourselves? Psalm 118 is intended as a book of instructions to answer these questions, to present guidance on how to live a godly and God-fearing life, approached in simplicity, sincerity, humility and faith: and thereby know His will.

In ancient times, this guidance was linked to the Hebrew alphabet, which has 22 letters, as a mnemonic vehicle, as if to offer the full gamut from Aleph to Tau - or "A to Z" as we would call it. Eight verses are assigned to each letter, for which reason it is referred to below as an octave. In the Hebrew text, each of the eight verses began with the respective letter of the octave. These Hebrew letters are missing from the Septuagint.

Set forth below, introducing the Church Fathers' commentaries on each octave, are St. Theophan the Recluse's comments on the Hebrew letters and their relationship to the overall theme of Psalm 118, as translated, summarized and paraphrased by F. Gleb. St. Theophan was deeply read in Patristics and in the Psalms, and this would seem to be the best means to cover this aspect. Ed.

Alleluia.

ALEPH*: 1. Blessed are the blameless in the way, who walk in the law of the Lord. 2. Blessed are they that search out His testimonies; with their whole heart shall they seek after Him. 3. For they that work iniquity have not walked in His ways. 4. Thou hast enjoined Thy commandments, that we should keep them most diligently. 5. Would that my ways were directed to keep Thy statutes. 6. Then shall I not be ashamed, when I look on all Thy commandments. 7. I will confess Thee with uprightness of heart, when I have learned the judgments of Thy righteousness. 8. I will keep Thy statutes; do not utterly forsake me.*

---

1. Presented here is Psalm 118 from the Septuagint in the version THE PSALTER ACCORDING TO THE SEVENTY, translated by Holy Transfiguration Monastery, Brookline, MA, by permission. Excerpts from the church fathers are from GRACE FOR GRACE: THE PSALTER AND THE HOLY FATHERS - see p. 154. In the KJV this is Psalm 119.

Octave 1, v. 1-8: ALEPH. Science, leader: the leading principles of a godly, god-pleasing life, the complete system of moral principles. The first three verses describe the degrees by which such a life attains perfection, the following two describe the productive powers of such a life: strong zeal and God's grace; the last three explain the conditions necessary for such a life.[2]

The order of expressions should not be neglected ...it is not first 'Blessed are they that search out His testimonies,' but 'Blessed are the blameless in the way.' Hence the primary condition is to enter into the way of truth with experienced moral conduct and oriented towards the seeking of a life without fault by the practice of the virtue normally known as probity. Then follows the scrutiny of the testimonies of God, and to have, for their searching out, a soul that has been purified and corrected. This order another prophet also does not forget, who says: 'Sow to yourselves for righteousness, reap in mercy; break up your fallow ground' (sic - cf. Hos. 10:12) ...It is not firstly our illumination that is prescribed, but the seeding, the sowing to ourselves ...or that we should make of our manner of life a seed, with a view to hoping for fruits, when subsequently we will have harvested that which was sowed; then we will be illuminated by the light of knowledge.

Such then is the first blessedness: blessed are those who are pure [blameless] in the way, not a random way, uncertain and full of error, but a way in which we 'walk in the law of the Lord' ...But we must not merely enter into this way; we must continue in it to the end. In fact, when we are 'in the way,' we have not yet attained the destination ...The blessed Paul says, 'Not as though I had already attained, or were already perfect: but I follow after, so that I may apprehend that for which also I am apprehended of Christ Jesus.' So he still walks, but he walks 'forgetting those things which are behind, and reaching forth unto those things which are before. I press toward the mark for the prize of the high calling of God in Christ Jesus' (Phil. 3:12, 13-14). And what is the way, whereon all mankind which treads it is blessed, the Lord has taught, saying, 'I am the Way' (Jn. 14:6).
St. Hilary of Poitiers. C[3] pp. 101-105.

[Blameless in the way] are those who have 'not walked in the counsel of the ungodly, nor stood in the way of sinners' (Ps. 1:1), but who have chosen

---

2. *Psalm 118/119* based on the Septuagint Version and commented by Bishop (St.) Theophan the Recluse, A Summary of this Russian Commentary and translated by F. Gleb. Holy Trinity Monastery, Jordanville, NY. By permission.

3. C = *Commentaire sur le Psaume 118*, Vol. I by St. Hilary of Poitiers, © Sources Chrétiennes, #344, Cerf, Paris 1988. By permission.

the law and the direction in which this leads. He calls 'blameless' not those who are entirely beyond reproach and fault, for those were reserved unto Christ, by Christ, to those who are participants with Him; for men, then, irreproachability will be judged according to their measure, after the indulgence of God and not after the exact observance of the ordinances.
Appolinaris of Laodicea. LCP[4] p. 189.

The 'testimonies' may also be the teachings of God, as witness was born of them by Him and by His truth ...
'Blessed,' then, 'are they that search out His testimonies,' and who 'with their whole heart ...seek after Him:' they are remote from all worldly preoccupations and approach God by their virtuous actions and their right thoughts. And it is good to proclaim happy not those who have walked, but those 'who walk.'
St. Didymus the Blind, LCP[4] pp. 193-195.

When you hear 'would that,' recognize the words of one wishing, and having recognized the expression of a wish, lay aside the pride of presumption. For who, saying that he desires, has it in his power to do without the help of God? Therefore if man desires what God charges, God must be beseeched to [facilitate] Himself what He directs [to be done] ... 'I will confess Thee with uprightness of heart' ...This is not a confession of sins, but of praise, as He also says in whom there was no sin, 'I will confess unto Thee, O Father, Lord of heaven and earth' (cf. Mt. 11:25).
Blessed Augustine of Hippo. OTP[5] (5, 6, 7) p. 560.

BETH: *9. Wherewithal shall a young man correct his way? By keeping Thy words. 10. With my whole heart have I sought after Thee, cast me not away from Thy commandments. 11. In my heart have I hid Thy sayings that I might not sin against Thee. 12. Blessed art Thou, O Lord, teach me Thy statutes. 13. With my lips have I declared all the judgments of Thy mouth. 14. In the way of Thy testimonies have I found delight, as much as in all riches. 15. On Thy commandments will I ponder, and I will understand Thy ways. 16. On Thy statutes will I meditate; I will not forget Thy words.*

---

4. LCP = *La Chaîne Palestinienne sur le Psaume 118*, Vol. I comprising various commentators from the third through the fifth centuries A.D. Precise details regarding individual sources are lacking. © Sources Chrétiennes, #189, Cerf, Paris 1972. By permission.

5. OTP = *On the Psalms* by Blessed Augustine of Hippo. Nicene and Post-Nicene Fathers, First Series, Vol. VIII, Wm. B. Eerdmans Publishing Co., Grand Rapids, MI. 1978.

Octave 2, v. 9-16: BETH. House, dwelling, abode: the will, the heart, feelings, taste and interest, meditation and memory - the whole human nature can become an abode for the commandments. What kind of abode shall we prepare for the commandments, and how shall we establish it in ourselves?[2]

Certainly it is desirable that every age bring some human vices forward for the inquiry into a life without fault, because it is profitable to correct oneself, even belatedly, in doing away with these vices. But for shaping a man who will please God, the Prophet does not wait until he will have been formed -- after a long and durable habit of faults -- for the instruction of God and the precepts of fear of Him. But he desires that those years which do not have the experience of sins, and the age that is still ignorant of them be formed, not only by intermittant aspirations for a life without fault, but also by the associated habit gained during adolescence. Indeed, it is difficult to renounce habits; it is hard to abstract oneself from things familiar ...Also the best worshipper of God will be not only he who has remitted his sins, even those rendered without intent, but those who are even in ignorance of vices would be assured of being without fault.

The prophet Jeremiah recollects the happiness of that age when he says: 'It is good for a man when he bears a yoke in his youth. He will sit alone, and be silent, because he has borne it upon him' (Lam. 3:27-28).

St. Hilary of Poitiers. C[3] pp. 127-129.

There is another mode of interpreting it, by recognizing in the expression the younger son in the Gospel (cf. Lk. 15:12ff), who returned to himself and said, 'I will arise and go to my father.' How did he correct his way except by ruling himself after the words of God, which he desired as one longing for his father's bread? ...

What is it to be cast away of God, save not to be aided? For human infirmity is not equal to obeying His righteous and exalted commandments, unless His love prevents and aids ...Teach me, he says, as those learn who do them, not as merely remembering them, so they may have something of which to speak ...We understand that there is no more speedy, no more sure, no shorter, no higher way of the testimonies of God than Christ, 'in whom are hid all the treasures of wisdom and knowledge' (Col. 2:3) ...Those are the testimonies by which He deigns to prove to us how much He loves us (cf. Rom. 5:8, 9).

Blessed Augustine of Hippo. OTP[5] (9, 10, 11, 13) pp. 561, 562.

Those who do not receive the instructions of God superficially sequester them in their heart for them to conform their thoughts to His intention, with the aim of being without sin before God, who sees those things

which are hidden .. With this verse, the words [of Solomon] are also in consonance: 'My son, if thou wilt receive the utterance of my commandment, and hide it with thee; thine ear shall hearken to wisdom' (Prov: 2:1).
St. Didymus the Blind. LCP[4] p. 209.

If one does not confine the commandments of God in his heart as a treasure, the Evil One will arrive and seize them.
St. Athanasius of Alexandria. LCP[4] p. 209.

He who lays hold of the consciousness of his progress since, with his whole heart, he searched out God, blesses God and gains grace from that time forward for that in which he has been judged worthy. Having indeed [acquired] secret and holy words to be hidden, he blesses the Lord according to their value; and he demands to have the Lord Himself for his master, for he wants to learn direction from His statutes.
Origen. LCP[4] p. 209.

The secret instructions I have hidden in my heart like mystical science; but these 'judgments' I have declared to all, for it behooves all men to hear them, because all ought to keep [awareness that we must all] 'appear before the judgment seat of Christ' (2 Cor. 5:10).
Eusebius of Caesaraea. LCP[4] p. 211.

One meditates on the statutes of God, not with words or beautiful phrases, but with their accomplishments after having understood them. 'For not the hearers of the law are just before God, but the doers of the law shall be justified' (Rom. 2:13).
Origen. LCP[4] p. 213.

GIMEL: *17. Give reward unto Thy servant, quicken me and I will keep Thy words. 18. O unveil mine eyes, and I shall perceive wondrous things out of Thy law. 19. I am a sojourner on the earth, hide not from me Thy commandments. 20. My soul hath longed to desire Thy judgments at all times. 21. Thou hast rebuked the proud; cursed are they that decline from Thy commandments. 22. Remove from me reproach and contempt, for after Thy testimonies have I sought. 23. For princes sat and they spake against me, but Thy servant pondered on Thy statutes. 24. For Thy testimonies are my meditation, and Thy statutes are my counsellors.*

Octave 3, v. 17-24: GIMEL. Camel: this is the most enduring of all pack animals. The psalm speaks of difficulties in the spiritual life and ways to overcome them. Those walking on the path of commandments are

111

likened to the camel, especially in the beginning, when they have not yet acquired the taste of it, but also later on when pressures of external troubles burden the inner disposition. All this is overcome by adherence to the given promise.[2]

Those who do not have a conscience assured of purity of heart cannot pray with the words of the Prophet 'Give reward unto Thy servant.' If, indeed, the reward is according to the measure of our works, we remain within the chastisement of our sins and our faults. It is already good if one has the means of assurance that permit thanks to God thus: 'Not according to our iniquities hath He dealt with us, neither according to our sins hath He rewarded us. For according to the height of heaven from the earth, the Lord hath made His mercy to prevail over them that fear Him ...for He knoweth whereof we are made' (Ps. 102: 9, 10, 12). It is important to recognize such mercy on the part of God for us, to know that we are insulated by the accustomed practice of our faults, and for us to begin to be worthy of the mercy of God.
St. Hilary of Poitiers. C[3] p. 147.

There are four modes of reward: either (1) evil for evil, as God will reward everlasting fire to the unrighteous, or (2) good for good, as He will reward an everlasting kingdom to the righteous, or (3) good for evil, as Christ by grace justifies the ungodly, or (4) evil for good, as Judas and the Jews through their wickedness persecuted Christ. Of these four modes of reward, the first two belong to justice ...the third to mercy ...the fourth God does not know, for to none does He reward evil for good. But that which I have placed third in order is in the first instance necessary, for unless God rewarded good for evil, there would be none to whom He could reward good for good.
Blessed Augustine of Hippo. OPS[5] (15), p. 562.

There is a particular virtue available to overcome all the other passions. But tedium [despondency of the spirit] is a kind of total death for the monk. A brave soul can stir up his dying mind, but tedium and laziness scatter every one of his treasures.
St. John Climacus. *The Ladder of Divine Ascent,*[6] Step 13. p. 163.

There is a very neat answer of Abbot Macarius to one who asked him why he was troubled with hunger as early as the third hour in the desert,

---

6. *The Ladder of Divine Ascent* by St. John Climacus, transl. by Colm Luibheid and Norman Russell, CWS © Paulist Press, Mahway, NJ 07430.

when in the monastery he had often scorned food for a whole week without feeling hungry. "Because," said he, "here there is nobody to see your fast, and feed and support you with his praise of you: but there you grew fat on the notice of others and the food of vainglory."

St. John Cassian. *Conference of Abbot Serapion,*[7] Chap. XII. NPNF, SS Vol. XI, p. 345.

As we pass from things visible to things unseen we shall be able to say with the Apostle: 'For we know that if our earthly house of this tabernacle were dissolved, we have a building of God, an house not made with hands, eternal in the heavens' (2 Cor. 5:1), and this also ...'For our conversation is in heaven, from whence also we look for the Saviour, the Lord Jesus Christ, who shall change our vile body that it may be fashioned like unto His glorious body' (Phil. 3:20, 21), and of this the blessed David: 'For I am a sojourner upon the earth' ...so that we may in accordance with the Lord's word be made like those of whom the Lord speaks to His Father in the gospel as follows: 'They are not of the world, as I am not of the world' (Jn. 17:16).

St. John Cassian. *Conference of Abbot Paphnutius.*[7] Ibid., p. 322.

The words 'I am a sojourner on the earth' cannot seem to have been said in reference to the body, since the body derives its origin from the earth. But in this most profound question I dare not define anything, for it might justly have been said in respect of the soul (which God forbid we should suppose derived from the earth) ...or in reference to the whole man, since he was at one time an inhabitant of Paradise ...or one to whom an everlasting country has been promised in heaven ...Those whose conversation is in heaven, as far as they abide here conversant, are in truth strangers. Let them pray therefore that the commandments of God may not be hidden from them, whereby they may be freed from this temporary sojourn, by loving God, with whom they will be for evermore.

Blessed Augustine of Hippo. OPS[5] (18, 19), pp. 562, 563.

Why then has he not said "my soul hath longed for Thy judgments," but 'my soul hath longed *to desire* Thy judgments'? ...It does not belong to all to desire the judgments of God at all times, but only to those who do not sin. Indeed, the moment I sin, if I desire the judgments, I desire to be chastised. It is the perfect man, therefore, to whom it belongs to desire the judgments at all times. It is for this reason the Prophet says the words as cited.

---

7. *The Conferences of St. John Cassian,* Nicene and Post-Nicene Fathers, Second Series, Vol. XI, Wm. B. Eerdmans Publishing Company, Grand Rapids, MI. 1978.

THE LAMENT OF EVE

Origen. LCP[4] pp. 219, 220.

The proud err from the commandments of God. For it is one thing not to fulfill the commandments of God through infirmity or ignorance, another to err from them through pride ...But consider now ...he does not say, "cursed are they that *have erred* from Thy commandments," so that only that sin of the first men should come to mind, but he says, 'Cursed are they that do err [decline].' For it was needful that all might be terrified by that example, so they might not err from the divine commandments, and by loving righteousness in all time, recover in the toil of this world, what we lost in the pleasure of Paradise.

Testimonies are called in Greek *martyria* ...whence those who on account of their testimony to Christ have been brought low by various sufferings, and have contended unto death for the truth ...When the body of Christ speaks in this way, does it consider it any punishment to hear rebuke and shame from the ungodly? ...It prays for its very enemies, to whom it sees it is destructive, to cast the holy name of Christ as a reproach to Christians ...Martyrdom in the name of Christ ...is not only not a disgrace, but a great ornament ...

Remember that among the statutes of the Lord there is none more difficult and more worthy of admiration, than that every man should love his enemies (cf. Mat. 5:44). Thus then the body of Christ was exercised, so that it meditated on the acts of martyrdom that testified of Him.

Blessed Augustine of Hippo. OTP[5] (21, 22, 23, 24), p. 563.

DALETH: *25. My soul hath cleaved unto the earth; quicken me according to Thy word. 26. My ways have I declared, and Thou hast heard me; teach me Thy statutes. 27. Make me to understand the way of Thy statutes, and I will ponder on Thy wondrous works. 28. My soul hath slumbered from despondency, strengthen me with Thy words. 29. Remove from me the way of unrighteousness, and with Thy law have mercy on me. 30. I have chosen the way of truth, and Thy judgments have I not forgotten. 31. I have cleaved to Thy testimonies, O Lord; put me not to shame. 32. The way of Thy commandments have I run, when Thou didst enlarge my heart.*

Octave 4, v. 25-32: DALETH. Door - doors leading to repentance and conversion. The Prophet takes the repentant sinner and with him recalls the road to conversion, from the first stimulation of the conscience to the decisive entry upon the path of commandments. The doors of repentance are in the first three verses, a transitional stage in the next two verses, and the doors into the righteous life in the last three. [2]

One can see here an allusion to his application to his prayer, how, because of the confession of his sins, the Prophet prostrates himself on the ground, being 'cleaved unto the earth' ... We are invited to understand that he regrets here the connection of his soul and body. There are still other good reasons which would make us think this sense is acceptable. In fact, the Apostle speaks of our 'vile body' (Phil. 3:21). The Prophet has also said: 'For our soul hath been humbled down to the dust' (Ps. 43:26).

St. Hilary of Poitiers. C[3] pp. 177-178.

That which declares itself is 'a sacrifice unto God ...a heart that is broken and humbled' (Ps. 50:17). This he says now to have accomplished: he has made his soul descend to the ground in order to say this; he has voluntarily humiliated himself.

Apollinaris of Laodicea. LCP[4] p. 231.

He seems to me to say this: I have confessed my sins, and You have heard me so that You would remit them. 'Teach me Thy statutes.' I have acknowledged my ways: You have blotted them out; teach me Yours. Teach me so I may act, not merely so I may know how I ought to act ...

Blessed Augustine of Hippo. OTP[5] (27, 28), p. 564.

In the same way as slumber is the commencement of sleep, one can also say of the soul, when she begins to sin, she is falling into slumber: she is lured as in sleep by sin, but she redresses and awakens herself by the remembrance of good. The more one examines oneself, the more one accuses oneself of this, in confession, as of a former fault. But if You give me to understand of Your statutes, I will be 'strengthened with Thy words.'

I have covered 'the way' a little of the time, he says, not just a single commandment, but all 'Thy commandments' while accomplishing by my works and in my deeds those things they ordain. This is why Paul -- who also accomplished the same, said: 'I have finished my course, I have kept the faith' (2 Tim. 4:7) ... Two conditions are indeed required: that the thorns of life do not choke 'the good seed' which is in us (cf. Mt. 13:7-22) and that we be helped by God.

Eusebius of Caesarea. LCP[4] p. 237, 243, 245.

The widening of the heart is the delight we take in righteousness. This is the gift of God, the effect of which is, that we are not straitened in His commandments through the fear of punishment, but widened through love, and the delight we have in righteousness.

Blessed Augustine of Hippo. OTP[5] (30), p. 564-656.

HE: *33. Set before me for a law, O Lord, the way of Thy statutes, and I will seek after it continually. 34. Give me understanding, and I will search out Thy law, and I will keep it with my whole heart. 35. Guide me in the path of Thy commandments, for I have desired it. 36. Incline my heart unto Thy testimonies and not unto covetousness. 37. Turn away mine eyes that I may not see vanity, quicken Thou me in Thy way. 38. Establish for Thy servant Thine oracle unto fear of Thee. 39. Remove my reproach which I have feared, for Thy judgments are good. 40. Behold, I have longed after Thy commandments; in Thy righteousness quicken me.*

Octave 5, v. 33-40: HE. Here: here is what has to be done. Seek from God the outline of the godly way (v. 33), knowledge (v. 34) and strength (v. 35). But no matter how much you ask for it, you will not get it if you do not apply your own efforts. Therefore seek (v. 33), safeguard (v. 34) and long for (v. 35) the way through the joint application of freedom and grace for a true and godly life. Compel yourself to every good deed, take care that your intentions are pure and unselfish (v. 36); do not get carried away by vanity (v. 37), let the fear of the Lord animate you. However, sinful thoughts will slip through; therefore let repentance be the background of your life (v. 39). Having done all this, put yourself into God's hands, striving only to please God (v. 40).[2]

What, then, would this law, 'the way of Thy statutes' be? ...When they traversed on foot across the Red Sea, the people who left Egypt received a kind of statute of the way which had been established for them by a judgment not human but divine (cf. Num. 33:1-2) ...But when God had decided that the people would stay for a long time in the same camp, neither the pillar of fire went before them by night, nor a pillar of a cloud preceded them by day. This was the law of the way which He established. And if we recall with care the stops and stages of the camp, as well as its conditions of installation, as defined in the Book of Exodus, we will see precisely the grand wonders of a celestial journey. It is why the Prophet has frequently prayed, saying: 'I shall perceive wondrous things out of Thy law' (v. 18).
St. Hilary of Poitiers. C[3] pp. 199, 201.

One is speaking who is growing in grace, and who knows that it is God's gift that he profit in grace ... Does 'continually' mean as long as we live here, because we progress in grace so long as we live here? ...Here the law of God is examined into, as long as we progress in it, both by knowing it and by loving it: but there its fulness abides for our enjoyment, not for our examination. So also is this spoken: 'Seek ye His face at all times' (Ps. 104:4). Where 'continually' except here? For there we will not 'seek' the face of God, when 'we shall see Him face to face' (cf. 1 Cor. 13:12) ...seek the law of God, that is, the truth of God: for in this very psalm it is said, 'And Thy law is truth' (v. 142) ... When each man has searched the law, and searched its deep things, in which its whole meaning consists, he ought indeed to love God with all his heart, with all his soul, with all his mind, and his neighbour as himself. 'For on these two commandments hang all the Law and the Prophets' (Mt. 22:37-40). This he seems to have promised when he said, 'I will keep it with my whole heart' (v. 34).

Blessed Augustine of Hippo. OTP[5] (32, 33, 34), p. 565.

When the heart of a man has attached itself passionately to evil from its youth (cf. Gen. 8:21), the man has a need for God to turn his heart towards righteousness, that is to say, God will direct our faculty of decision-making in the manner in which He organizes events and by the illumination of the Holy Spirit.

Apollinaris of Laodicia. LCP[4] p. 253.

Vanity and truth are directly contrary to one another. The desires of this world are vanity: but Christ, who frees us from the world, is truth. He is the way, too, wherein this man wishes to be quickened, for He is also the life: 'I am the way, the truth, and the life' (Jn. 14:6) are His own words ...

If it be a vain thing to do good works for the sake of men's praises, how much more vain for the sake of getting money, or increasing it, or retaining it, and any other temporal advantage which comes to us from outside? ...

What then do the words, 'Remove my reproach which I have feared' (v. 39) mean? The meaning of them must be derived from the former verse, since as long as a man does not turn away his eyes lest they behold vanity, he suspects in others what is going on in himself, so that he believes another to worship God, or do good works, from the same motive as himself. For men can see what we do, but with a view to what end we act is hidden.

Blessed Augustine of Hippo. OTP[5] (37, 38, 39, 40). Ibid.

It is not the word of a man who has a consciousness of having sinned, but that of a man who has dread [of sin], as in the phrase: 'From my secret sins cleanse me' (Ps. 18:12); I have confidence You will remove the reproach which I dread, for I am persuaded that Your judgments abound in the grace of your love for mankind.

St. Didymus the Blind. LCP[4] p. 257.

VAU: *41. Let Thy mercy come also upon me, O Lord, even Thy salvation according to Thy word. 42. So shall I give an answer to them that reproach me, for I have hoped in Thy words. 43. And take not utterly out of my mouth the word of truth, for in Thy judgments have I hoped. 44. So shall I keep Thy law continually, for ever, and unto the ages of ages. 45. And I walked in spa-*

ciousness, for after Thy commandments have I sought. 46. And I spake of Thy testimonies before kings, and I was not ashamed. 47. And I meditated on Thy commandments which I have greatly loved. 48. And I lifted up my hands to Thy commandments which I have loved, and I pondered on Thy statutes.

Octave 6, v. 41-48: VAU. Hook, anchor: an anchor is used to hold a boat securely, despite waves. The anchor is a symbol of hope and trust ...The first four verses describe the basis of hope: the unerring word of God's promises (v. 41, 42), God's judgments towards the godly and the wicked (v. 43, 44). The last four describe the state when hope has entered the heart: spaciousness of walk, fearless proclamation of truth, the seeking of the needful good part (cf. Lk. 10:42), and patient abiding in godliness.[2]

The Apostle desires us to be understood as the children of promise (cf. Rom 9:8): so we may not imagine that what we are is our own work, but refer the whole to the grace of God ...Christ Himself is the Salvation of God, so that the whole body of Christ may say, 'By the grace of God I am what I am' (1 Cor. 15:10) ...

Those to whom Christ crucified is a stumbling-block or foolishness (cf. 1 Cor. 1:23) reproach us with Him; ignorant that 'The Word was made flesh, and dwelt among us' (Jn. 1:14), the Word which 'was in the beginning,' and 'was with God, and was God' (Jn. 1:1). But although they may not reproach us with the Word which is unknown unto them, because His Divinity is not known to those by whom His weakness on the Cross is despised, let us nevertheless make answer of the Word, and let us not be terrified or confounded by their reproaches. For 'if they had known' the Word, 'they would not have crucified the Lord of glory' (1 Cor. 2:8) ...Therefore when the Psalmist had said, 'So shall I give an answer to them that reproach me,' he immediately adds, 'for I have hoped in Thy words,' which means exactly, in Thy promises.

Blessed Augustine of Hippo. OTP[5] (42, 43), pp. 566-567.

Numerous, according to the Apostle, are those who, after the 'wisdom of the world,' have 'rejected the wisdom of God;' also 'God made foolish the wisdom of the world' (cf. 1 Cor 1:19-21). What is indeed more foolish than the unbelief of those who, in an error well known by men without religion, add, moreover, the impious audacity to think that the divine words of the Scriptures do not have the coherence of a perfect teaching? And as, by reason of the impiety of their intellect, they cannot receive the divine words, in order to excuse their dulled wit, they abandon themselves to insults against the celestial works. They say they are totally unreasonable, imperfect, and pretend that their own propositions are the only ones that are smart and polished by the instruction of true wisdom, refuting in God, in

their foolishness, that which they have the audacity to attribute to themselves!
St. Hilary of Poitiers. C[3] pp. 225, 227.

He says this because those who have already received the 'word of truth' risk losing it, God taking it from their mouth, if they, having already received it, and already teach it, render themselves unworthy of this word. Also it has rightly been said: 'Neglect not the gift that is in thee' (1 Tim. 4:14), neglect being not only to fail to cultivate the grace and not making it grow, but equally not to conform one's life to it.
Origin. LCP[4] p. 263.

We have need of aid and succour from God to preserve the truth "definitively" and for our mouth not to hesitate between truth and falsehood; it is with purpose that he demands to maintain this behaviour, since he is guarding in his memory the judgments of God so as to find them in [times of] anguish. I well know, indeed, that if I am purified of all wrong opinion, 'I shall keep Thy law continually, for ever, and unto the ages of ages' without hindrance.
Eusebius of Caesarea. LCP[4] p. 265.

The Prophet does not fear any end to his life. In fact, his faith is not limited by the ages, but having a duty to guard the law, it is stretched into an infinity of time ... God said to Moses, 'Go, do all following the pattern which was showed thee on the mount.' He hastens, therefore, towards the laws of the 'everlasting ages' (cf. Isa. 24:5) In effect, if the 'Law' is a 'shadow of good things to come' (cf. Heb. 10:1), it is necessary that the body of the true Law be eternal.
St. Hilary of Poitiers. C[3] p. 233.

ZAIN: *49. Remember Thy words to Thy servant, wherein Thou hast made me to hope. 50. This hath comforted me in my humiliation, for Thine oracle hath quickened me. 51. The proud have transgressed exceedingly, but from Thy law have I not declined. 52. I remembered Thy judgments of old, O Lord, and was comforted. 53. Despondency took hold upon me because of the sinners who forsake Thy law. 54. Thy statutes were my songs in the place of my sojourning. 55. I remembered Thy name in the night, O Lord, and I kept Thy law. 56. This hath happened unto me because I sought after Thy statutes.*

Octave 7, v. 49-56: ZAIN. Olive: oil is made from the olive tree; it is the symbol of God's mercy and of all that is comforting and soothing. Assembled here are sayings which express grief of the soul and ways to its consolation: grief from the slowness of God's promises (v. 49), humiliating circumstances in life (v. 50), arrogance and mockeries of enemies (v. 51, 52), increase of sin and impiety (v. 53), weariness of the stay on earth (v. 54), and in all these afflictions, consolation is sought from God and His holy law (v. 55, 56).[2]

In pronouncing a "word" of promise, You have given us wings to hope in You and to despise the present; because I have desired the things celestial and seek the things eternal, I have struggled, I have contended, remembering this 'word.'
Origen. LCP[4] p. 271.

And which 'words' does he want God to 'remember', save the promise He gave them to be 'with you always' (Mt. 28:20), which made for them a consolation in persecutions.
St. Athanasius of Alexandria. LCP[4] p. 271.

Our Lord Himself says with His own lips: 'For whosoever exalteth himself shall be abased; and he that humbleth himself shall be exalted' (Lk. 14:11 and 18:14). We well understand here also that humiliation, not whereby each man humbles himself by confessing his sins, and by not arrogating righteousness to himself, but when each man is humbled by some tribulation or mortification which his pride deserved, or when he is exercised and proved by endurance (cf. Ecclus. 2:4, 5). Following on this, a little later this psalm says: 'Before I was humbled, I transgressed' (v. 67) ...
And the Lord Jesus, when He foretold that this humiliation would be brought upon His disciples by their persecutors, did not leave them without a hope, but gave them one, whereby they might find comfort in these words: 'In your patience shall ye possess your souls;' and declared even of their very bodies, which might be put to death by their enemies, and seemingly be utterly annihilated, that not a hair of their heads should perish (cf. Lk. 21:17, 18). This hope was given to Christ's Body, that is, to the Church, that it might be a comfort to her in her humiliation ...This hope He gave in the prayer which He taught us, where He enjoined us to say, 'Lead us not into temptation' (Mt. 6:13): for He in a manner implicitly promised that He would give to His disciples in their danger that which He taught them to ask for in their prayers. And indeed this Psalm is rather to be understood to speak of this hope: 'For Thy word hath quickened me.'
Blessed Augustine of Hippo. OTP[5] (51), p. 568.

EPILOGUE PART III: THE WAY, THE TRUTH AND THE LIFE

His own merits do not suffice to guarantee for our Prophet the hope of eternal life -- neither having put his hope in the word of God, nor in being consoled in this same hope, nor in having been quickened by the word of God, nor in not deviating from the law, nor being encouraged by the remembrance of His judgments -- he is still touched by the suffering occasioned by human impiety, and oppressed by the impious injustices of mankind. Indeed, every time a saint is beaten, he sympathizes with the humiliation -- the humiliation not only of him who is beaten, but also in the arrogance of him who does the beating ...Now, 'whether one member suffer, all the members suffer with it' (1 Cor. 12:26). This is why 'despondency took hold' upon the Prophet before the sinners who forsake the law of God: he is overwhelmed by a feeling of pity and of sadness and as if his own members had been in part sick from the danger which affects men who are unjust and irreligious.
St. Hilary of Poitiers. C^3 pp. 249, 251.

CHETH: *57. Thou art my portion, O Lord; I said that I would keep Thy law. 58. I entreated Thy countenance with my whole heart: Have mercy on me according to Thy word. 59. I have thought on Thy ways, and I have turned my feet back to Thy testimonies. 60. I made ready, and I was not troubled, that I might keep Thy commandments. 61. The cords of sinners have entangled me, but Thy law have I not forgotten. 62. At midnight I arose to give thanks unto Thee for the judgments of Thy righteouesness. 63. I am a partaker with all them that fear Thee, and with them that keep Thy commandments. 64. The earth, O Lord, is full of Thy mercy; teach me Thy statutes.*

Octave 8, v. 57-64: CHETH. Sin: The Prophet does not speak here about sin proper, but about how a sinner frees himself from its bondage, and what means he uses to stay on the right path. The sinner is taken at that very moment when awakening from sin he resolves to stop sinning. Before him are the world with its delights and the Lord with His commandments. Having considered the one and the other, he chooses the law (v. 57). However, old habits are not easily overcome, and he asks help from God (v. 58). Having received God's forgiveness, he considers a new life (v. 59), yet this decision does not make him a different person on the spot; he has to withstand and overcome sin (v. 60), and drop his former sinful friendships (v. 61). The Prophet offers powerful means to achieve this: nightly prayer (v. 62), contact with God-fearing people (v. 63), and the handing over of one's fate to the mercy of God (v. 64).[2]

Rare are those who have sufficient assurance to dare to say that God is 'their portion.' It requires renunciation of the world and all its affairs for God to be our portion for us. But should ambition come to monopolize us, the care of money occupy us, the attraction of pleasures seize us, the administration of our affairs stop us, then God will not be our portion if we are monopolized by the cares and the vices of this world that possess us.

As Moses received the order to reportion his habitation among the twelve tribes of the sons of Israel, concerning the tribe of Levi, he received this prescription: 'Therefore the Levites have no part nor inheritance among their brethren; the Lord Himself is their inheritance' (Deut. 10:9). And we recall that, again, it is written: 'And the Lord said to Aaron, Thou shalt have no inheritance in their land, neither shalt thou have any portion among them; for I am thy portion and thine inheritance in the midst of the children of Israel' (Num. 18:20).

Peter also, this herald of the Gospel, remember he had no portion of property among men when he replied to those who asked for alms: 'Silver and gold have I none; but such as I have give I thee' (Acts. 3:6). How beautiful, Peter, having renounced your possessions, when you say to your Lord: 'Behold, we have forsaken all, and followed Thee; what shall we have therefore? And Jesus said unto them, 'Verily I say unto you, That ye which have followed Me in the regeneration when the Son of man shall sit in the throne of His glory, ye also shall sit upon twelve thrones, judging the twelve tribes of Israel' (Mt. 19:27-28).

St. Hilary of Poitiers. C[3] pp. 259, 261.

The countenance of God is 'the express image of His person' (Heb. 1:3) as we have often said. Those who desire it, do so with their 'whole heart,' so that it is possible to contemplate it with a purified heart, and so that, having fixed their gaze on it, they could then say these words as presented. Consider how great are those who will see the face of God. As Jesus has taught you, to whom He has said: 'Blessed are the pure in heart, for they shall see God' (Mt. 5:8).

St. Didymus the Blind. LCP[4] pp. 281, 283.

A sensible sick man could say equally well to his doctor: "Take pity on me, according to your instruction: take care of me, as your discipline prescribes." He who makes this demand knows the manner in which this care will be exercised. Often, indeed, God assures our salvation by His correction. The chastisement comes because God loves mankind.

Theodoret of Cyrus. LCP[4] p. 283.

What are the 'cords' save bad thoughts and evil powers suggested by them, to try thereby to throw the righteous from their stability in God? ...The difficulties the sinners raise up against the just can also be their 'cords,' but in these the just also bear with them with valiance, when they have not forgotten the law of God. And those who are inviting a just man to sin by their deceiving words, surround him with 'cords,' but if he is vigilant, he will not forget the law of God.

St. Didymus the Blind. LCP[4], p. 265.

That the cords of the ungodly surround the righteous, is one of the righteous judgments of God. On this account the Apostle Peter says: 'The time is come that judgment must begin at the house of God' (1 Pet. 4:17). For he says this of the persecutions which the Church suffered, when the bands of the ungodly surrounded them. I suppose, therefore, that by 'midnight' we should understand the heavier seasons of tribulation. In which he said, 'I arose': since He did not so afflict him as to cast him down, but tried him, so that he arose, that is, that through this very tribulation he might advance to a bolder confession.

Blessed Augustine of Hippo. OTP[5] (60), p. 570.

The perfect [man] is, so to speak, a partaker of Christ, after the words: 'For we are made partakers of Christ' (Heb. 3:14); but our man, a beginner as he is, says that he is 'a partaker with them that fear' the Lord, and not merely those who fear, but of those who, because they fear, 'keep the commandments' of God. The mark of fear of God is to keep His commandments ...Prophetically he announces the future in saying 'the earth ...is full' of men fearing the Lord. Those, he says, will not have any other cause for 'Thy mercy,' for You acted in them with mercy when You gave Yourself up to them as teacher of mankind.

St. Athanasius of Alexandria. LCP[4] p. 291.

TETH: *65 Thou hast dealt graciously with Thy servant, O Lord, according to Thy word. 66. Goodness and discipline and knowledge teach Thou me, for in Thy commandments have I believed. 67. Before I was humbled, I transgressed; therefore Thy sayings have I kept. 68. Thou art good, O Lord, and in Thy goodness teach me Thy statutes. 69. Multiplied against me hath been the unrighteousness of the proud; but as for me, with my whole heart will I search out Thy commandments. 70. Curdled like milk is their heart; but as for me, in Thy law have I meditated. 71. It is good for me that Thou hast humbled me, that I might learn Thy statutes. 72. The law of Thy mouth is better to me than thousands of gold and silver.*

Octave 9, v. 65-72: TETH. Mud, clay: mud means dirt, but mud can be used for healing and out of clay are made useful vessels. In a similar way the Lord fashions the soul through various means. They are: God's grace and word (v. 65, 66), a sorrowful or happy life (v. 67, 68), with the Lord's consent, persecution from men (v. 69, 70), and the conviction that all this is under God's direct influence, and as such, the highest good for man (v. 71, 72).

In the preceding octave it has been shown how a sinner is pulled away from sin and turns to God, here it is shown how man's inner perfection is fashioned by the Lord through external circumstances of life.[2]

According to the Apostle, God has both goodness and severity (cf. Rom. 11:22): His goodness addresses those who rest firmly in the Faith, the severity in those who distance themselves from it. And since the saint has been confirmed in the Faith, he says: 'Thou hast dealt graciously with Thy servant' ...Also, as he wants to understand the reasonable and wise character of this goodness, he asks for no other master than God to teach him, in order that, at the same time he should learn 'discipline' and 'knowledge.' He calls 'discipline' the moral virtue, and 'knowledge' the intellectual virtue. In the same way, the phrase of the Proverbs should be recalled: 'Receive instruction, and not silver; and knowledge rather than tried gold' (Prov. 8:10).
St. Didymus the Blind. LCP[4] p. 293.

He prays these things may be increased and perfected. For those who said, 'Lord, increase our faith' (Lk. 17:5) had faith. And as long as we live in this world, these are the words of those who are making progress ...Now the word discipline, for which the Greeks use *paideia*, is employed in Scripture, where instruction through tribulation is to be understood: according to the words: 'Whom the Lord loveth He chasteneth, and scourgeth every son whom He receiveth' (Heb. 12:6) ...He, therefore, toward whom the Lord deals in goodness, that is, he in whom He mercifully inspires delight in that which is good, ought to pray instantly that this gift may be so increased in him, that he may not only despise all other delights in comparison with it, but also that he may endure any amount of suffering for its sake. Thus is discipline healthfully added to goodness ...

We undertake to obey commandments so we may deserve to receive promises ...Teach me goodness, therefore, by inspiring charity, teach me discipline by giving patience, teach me knowledge by enlightening my understanding: 'for in Thy commandments have I believed.' I have believed that You are God, who gives to man that which enables him to do as You command.
Blessed Augustine of Hippo. OTP[5]: (63, 65), p. 570, 571.

Abandoned because of my sins which I have committed previously, he says, I have been humbled, and that by the judgment of the Lord; that is why for me, who has been delivered for correction, I have need of teaching in order to understand the humiliation that has come to me, that came by design, out of goodness and for correction.

St. Athanasius of Alexandria. LCP[4]: p. 295.

Though we do not receive, let us persevere so we may receive; and if we do receive, then because we have received. For it is not at all His wish to defer giving, but by such delay He is contriving for us to persevere. With this intent He also lengthens out our supplication, and at times permits a temptation to come upon us, so we may continually flee for refuge to Him, and where we have fled for refuge, may there abide ...For this reason the Prophet also says, 'It is good for me that Thou hast humbled me.' And He Himself likewise said to the apostles, 'In the world ye shall have tribulation' (Jn. 16:33). And Paul signifies this self-same thing, when he says: 'There was given to me a thorn in the flesh, the messenger of Satan to buffet me' (2 Cor. 12:7), which is why when he sought to be delivered from the temptation, he failed to obtain relief, by reason of the great benefit ensuing from it.

And if we would go over the whole life of David, we will find him more glorious in his dangers, both he himself and all the others like him. For so Job at that season shone forth the more abundantly, and Joseph too in this way became the more approved, and Jacob also, and his father likewise, and his father's father, and as many as ever put on crowns of peculiar glory, it was by tribulations and temptations that they first won their crowns, then had their names recited.

Being conscious of all these things, according to the wise saying, let us 'not make haste in time of trouble' (cf. Ecclus. 2:2), but let us teach ourselves one thing only, how to bear all nobly, and not to be curious or inquisitive about any of the things that are coming to pass. For to know when our tribulations should be done away belongs to God, who permits them to befall us, but to bear them, brought upon us, with all thankfulness, all that is the work of a good disposition on our part; and if this be so, then all our blessings will follow.

St. John Chrysostom. *Homily X on Matthew III*, (8), NPNF, FS Vol. X, p. 67.

JOD: *73. Thy hands have made me and fashioned me; give me understanding and I will learn Thy commandments. 74. They that fear Thee shall see me and be glad, for on Thy words have I set my hope. 75. I have known, O Lord, that Thy judgments are righteousness, and with truth hast Thou humbled me. 76. Let now Thy mercy be my comfort, according to Thy saying unto Thy servant. 77. Let Thy compassions come upon me and I shall live, for Thy law is my meditation. 78. Let the proud be put to shame, for unjustly have they transgressed against me; but as for me, I will ponder on Thy commandments. 79. Let those that fear Thee return unto me, and those that know*

Thy testimonies. 80. Let my heart be blameless in Thy statutes, that I may not be put to shame.

Octave 10, v. 73-80: JOD. Hand: the hand is the symbol of God's Al-mightiness. He created everything. He keeps everything in His hands and provides. Mentioned here is the creation of man by God and the ability to understand one's destination (v. 73, 74) in circumstances shaped by God's hands for our salvation. Made wise by subduing circumstances (v. 75), the Prophet prays for divine mercy to descend and alter his destiny relying on God's words (v. 76) with the aid of divine animation (v. 77), for the sake of putting to shame the haughty sinners (v. 78) and communion with the godly (v. 79), but most of all for the shaping of a heart blameless in God's statutes.[2]

God does not fashion in the way of a potter ...but as an artisan imple-ments in creating, accomplishing by his power a realization of a particular form. And He is wont to produce in the initial creation, anciently formu-lated concepts of which it is said: 'Before I formed thee in the belly I knew thee' (Jer. 1:5) ...Paul also says, 'Consider what I say; and the Lord give thee understanding in all things' (2 Tim. 2:7). This request addressed to the Creator is logical. It implies: tend to Your creation for it to achieve its con-templated being by giving it the [necessary] intelligence, and that which You have prepared for it to live in closeness to you, make it live in intimacy with You by the knowledge of Your will.
Appolinaris of Laodicea. LCP[4] pp. 305, 307.

Let them understand by the hands of God the power and wisdom of God, both of which titles are given to Christ (cf. 1 Cor. 1:24), who is also understood under the figure, Arm of the Lord (cf. Isa. 53:1). Or let them understand by the hands of God, the Son and the Holy Spirit, since the Holy Spirit works conjointly with the Father and the Son, as the Apostle says: 'But all these worketh that one and the self-same Spirit' (1 Cor. 12:11)
...'For on Thy words have I set my hope,' that is, the things which You have promised so they may be the sons of promise, the seed of Abraham, in whom all nations are blessed (cf. Gen. 12:3 and 26:4). Who are those who fear God, and whom will they see and be glad, for on His words has he set his hope? Whether it be the body of Christ, that is, the Church, whose words these are through Christ, or within it, and concerning it, these are as it were the words of Christ concerning Himself ...The same persons who see the Church and are glad, are the Church ...
For then indeed I shall truly live, when I shall not be able to fear lest I die. This is styled life absolutely and without any addition, nor is any life save that which is everlasting and blessed understood, as though it alone

were to be called life; compared with it, that which we now lead ought rather to be called death than life, according to those words in the Gospel: 'If thou wilt enter into life, keep the commandments' (Mt. 19:17).
Blessed Augustine of Hippo. OTP[5] (77), p. 572.

CAPH: 81. My soul fainteth for Thy salvation; on Thy words have I set my hope. 82. Mine eyes are grown dim with waiting for Thine oracle; they say: When wilt Thou comfort me? 83. For I am become like wine-skin in the front; yet Thy statutes have I not forgotten. 84. How many are the days of Thy servant? When wilt Thou execute judgment for me on them that persecute me? 85. Transgressors have told me fables, but they are not like Thy law, O Lord. 86. All Thy commandments are truth. Without a cause have men persecuted me; do Thou help me. 87. They well nigh made an end of me on the earth; but as for me, I forsook not Thy commandments. 88. According to Thy mercy quicken me, and I will keep the testimonies of Thy mouth.

Octave 11, v. 81-88: CAPH. Palm of the hand: The palm can slap or caress. The Prophet here presents a person insulted, pressed by injustice and appealing to God for aid. What is described here is very much relevant to Job, the martyrs, and to all who struggle against sin and the passions. We have here a short course on how to find the strength and the capability in the endless struggle against the difficulties in spiritual life.[2]

In a very logical way, wanting to explain what is 'salvation,' he elaborates, saying 'on Thy words have I set my hope': he desires to signify that 'Thy salvation,' is the Son of God.
Eusebius of Caesarea. LCP[4] p. 319.

There is also a fainting that is laudable or desirable ...For it is said of a good failing: 'My soul longeth and fainteth for the courts of the Lord' (Ps. 83:1). So also here he does not say, faints away from Thy salvation, but 'fainteth for Thy salvation,' that is towards Thy salvation. This losing ground is therefore good, for it indicates a longing after good, not yet gained indeed, but most eagerly and earnestly desired. But who says this except the chosen generation, the royal priesthood, the holy nation, the peculiar people (cf. 1 Pet. 2:9), longing for Christ from the origin of the human race even unto the end of this world, in the persons of those who, each in his own time, have lived, are living, or are to live here? ...The first seasons of the Church, therefore, had saints, before the Virgin's delivery, who desired the advent of His Incarnation, but these times, since He has ascended into heaven, have saints who desire His manifestation to judge the quick and the dead.
Blessed Augustine of Hippo. OTP[5] (81), p. 573.

One also calls 'teaching' the divine inspired Scriptures. Consequently, those who 'faint' are not only those who await the divine promise and who hope for the end of evil by which they are menaced: it is also those who read the divine teaching, who aspire to grasp its sense exactly, that find in this discovered consolation an appeasement for their soul.
Theodoret of Cyrus. LCP[4] p. 321.

'According to Thy mercy quicken me.' This was not to be passed over in silence, on account of that sweetest name of martyrs, who beyond doubt when such great cruelty of the persecutors was raging that the Church almost came to an end upon earth, would never have kept the testimonies of God, unless that had been vouchsafed them which is here spoken of: 'According to Thy mercy quicken me.' For they were quickened, lest by loving life, they should deny the life, and by denying it, should lose it: and thus they who for life refused to forsake the truth, lived by dying for the truth.
Blessed Augustine of Hippo. OTP[5] (84, 88), pp. 574, 575.

He claims not to have been delivered from the hands of his enemies until well nigh death: it is not a request for eternal life, but for the present life. He is not asking for it as an end in itself, but for how much it will contribute towards an end that is good. But as for me, he says, I will keep the ordinances of God, thanks to which, precisely, eternal life is acquired ...
Another says: He calls 'commandments' the promises. Full of confidence, he says, in Your promises and their truth, I seek the succour that comes from You, my God.
Apollinaris of Laodicea. LCP[4] p. 329.

He has avoided the words of abasement: he has not demanded life in exchange for his righteousness, but he beseeches to obtain it as a gift of the 'mercy' of God, promising himself to 'keep the testimonies' of God.
Theodoret of Cyrus. LCP[4] p. 329.

LAMED: *89. For ever, O Lord, Thy word abideth in heaven. 90. Unto generation and generation is Thy truth; Thou hast laid the foundation of the earth, and it abideth. 91. By Thine ordinance doth the day abide, for all things are Thy servants. 92. If Thy law had not been my meditation, then should I have perished in my humiliation. 93. I will never forget Thy statutes, for in them hast Thou quickened me. 94. I am Thine, save me; for after Thy statutes have I sought. 95. Sinners have waited for me to destroy me; but Thy testimonies have I understood. 96. Of all perfection have I seen the outcome; exceeding spacious is Thy commandment.*
Octave 12, v. 89-96: LAMED. To teach: to teach others or to teach oneself. Here, of course, the latter is meant: to learn to understand God's

will and to act in accordance with it. In heaven and on earth everything complies with the will of God (v. 89-91), and we should do likewise. Acting thus, we will not perish under humbling circumstances (v. 92); behaving in accordance with God's statutes we will be quickened (v. 93); seeking them, we will feel God's protection over us (v. 94). The understanding of God's testimonies will teach us how to avoid enemies (v. 95), and at last the entry upon the path of God's will give spaciousness and freedom (v. 96).[2]

He develops and addresses some more elevated dogmas. He makes mention of the eternal Word of the Father, and not solely 'In the beginning was the Word' (Jn. 1:1). He speaks also of the order of the universe, clearly designating the creation in its entirety as His 'servants' [By Thine Ordinance doth the day abide, for all things are Thy servants - v. 91].
St. Athanasius of Alexandria. LCP[4] p. 333.

The man who speaks in this psalm, as if he were tired of human mutability, whence this life is full of temptations, among his tribulations ...burning with longings for the heavenly Jerusalem, looked up to the realms above, and said, 'For ever, O Lord, Thy word abideth in heaven,' that is, among Thy angels who serve everlastingly in Thine armies, without desertion ...Beholding therefore the earth next after heaven with the gaze of a faithful mind, he finds in it generations which are not in heaven and says: 'Unto generation and generation is Thy truth' (v. 90), signifying all generations by this expression, from which the Truth of God was never absent in His saints.
Blessed Augustine of Hippo. OTP[5] (89, 90). p. 575.

The generations that have received the truth of God are two in number: the Jewish people who possess the law and the prophets, and the Church of Christ. Now the 'truth' of God is not for *some* generations to generations, but for *one* 'generation' firstly and *one* generation' in the second [mention]. With regard to other people, they are in a state of error. When the first generation had rejected the truth and had said, [as it were], 'Away with such a fellow from the earth' (cf. Acts 22:22), 'the Truth' passed from that generation to the other generation. On that Truth, the earth is founded. On that stone, on that corner stone as a foundation (cf. Eph. 2:20) are built all those on earth who are saved. That precisely is why it 'abides' on earth.
Origen. LCP[4] p. 333.

It is good that there exists a unique epitome of virtue, a term that belongs at the end of progress completed, for each moment of progress short of its immediate end. This, then, which attains the limit of virtue after having passed through all the stages of progress, of this is said: 'Of all perfection have I seen the outcome,' for he has overcome well the starts and well the limits while he lifted himself up towards perfect good. The limit of the improvement which presented itself at the outset is the beginning of that which made him succeed, and the expression of this is the initial element of the [steps] to follow. That is why it is said, 'When a man hath done, then he beginneth' (Ecclus. 18:7).

St. Didymus the Blind. LCP[4] p. 341.

MEM: *97. O how I have loved Thy law, O Lord! the whole day long it is my meditation. 98. Above mine enemies hast Thou made me wise in Thy commandments, for it is mine for ever. 99. Above all that teach me have I gained understanding, for Thy testimonies are my meditation. 100. Above mine elders have I received understanding, for after Thy commandments have I sought. 101. From every way that is evil have I restrained my feet that I might keep Thy words. 102. From Thy judgments have I not declined, for Thou hast set a law for me. 103. How sweet to my palate are Thy sayings! more sweet than honey to my mouth. 104. From Thy commandments have I gained understanding; therefore have I hated every way of unrighteousness.*

Octave 13, v. 97-104: MEM. Spot, blot, vice, moral imperfection, sin. This octave reveals how defects of the soul are reformed: blindness of the mind, corruption of the will, roughness of the heart, insensibility. A life in conformance with the law opens the eyes of the mind, which then understands everything clearly (v. 97 to 100); it restores righteousness to the will and regulates all its moves (v. 101, 102). In the heart it quickens the repressed feeling to all that is holy and installs a revulsion to all that is evil.[2]

Love is therefore the breadth of the commandment. For how can it be that what God commends to be loved should be loved, and yet the commandment itself be not loved? ...By such love lust is driven out: lust, which repeatedly opposes our performing the commandments of the law, when 'the flesh lusteth against the spirit' (Gal. 5:17).

Blessed Augustine of Hippo. OTP[5] (97), p. 576.

The law considers not only the language and the word, but also the deeds ...Now in this passage, he has said 'the whole day long it is my meditation,' but in the first psalm, it is not only the day, it is also the night in which he who desires to become blessed should meditate on the law, it is said (cf. Ps. 1:2). Why, then, has he omitted to name the night? Is there a difference between these two formulations? He has already said that here below the life of men is mixed: for here below we know both a day and a night, but when we will be saints and blessed, the night will not come to take us on its tour, we will just be in the day. Let us remark also that perhaps the faithful or one that is progressing [in the faith] may no longer simply lead their life now by day and now by night: in the day, when he accomplishes the obligations prescribed by the law, or in the night when he does not continue to fulfill the law with all his heart on that on which he meditates, or even when he frets contrarily at his duties.

Origen. LCP[4] p. 345.

The invisible enemies that oppress me seek with great zest to make me prefer pleasure. This pleasure provokes malcontentment before all arduous work, to the point that one even plans to abandon the divine commandment which is being carried out with great effort. But stronger than pleasure and than our enemies which are extolling it, is that which has been given by God if one is 'wise in Thy commandment,' while pleasure is of short duration and transient. That is why, in his hymn of gratitude, addressing God, he said: 'Thou made me wise in Thy commandment,' from which it follows also that I am 'above mine enemies.'

St. Didymus the Blind. LCP[4] p. 349.

After having confessed that he loves the divine law with a burning love, the Prophet returns all to divine grace: it is from You, he says, that I have received the wisdom and the knowledge that causes me to love Your law, for You have given me understanding above that of my enemies. That is why they seek to kill me while I refuse to revenge myself on those who assault me, for I dream of the eternal reward for virtue.

Theodoret of Cyrus, LCP[4] p. 349.

The characteristic of a sovereign is to instruct; to be instructed is the part of his subjects. Saul reigned, and moreover he was older. Yet neither his obligation as king nor his age had rendered him wise; to the contrary he desired to kill his benefactor. The great David himself, who was still in the number of those who obeyed and was at a young age, loved philosophy and neither supported being the first to engage in unjust combat nor revenging himself on those who made violence against him.

Theodoret of Cyrus. LCP[4] p. 353.

(The psalmist) puts well in evidence the free character of his will when he says: 'I have restrained my feet.' He pronounces this verse thinking that it is in his power to set his feet on a walk astray. That is in accord with this other text: 'Turn away from evil, and do good' (Ps. 33:14), for he who distances himself from evil, restrains his feet 'from every way that is evil,' so that effecting the good, he might keep the words of God.

St. Didymus the Blind. LCP[4] p. 335.

NUN: *105. Thy law is a lamp unto my feet and a light unto my paths. 106. I have sworn and resolved that I will keep the judgments of Thy righteousness. 107. I was humbled exceedingly; O Lord, quicken me according to Thy word. 108. The free-will offerings of my mouth be Thou now pleased to receive, O Lord, and teach me Thy judgments. 109. My soul is in Thy hands continually, and Thy law have I not forgotten. 110. Sinners have set a snare for me, yet from Thy commandment have I not strayed. 111. I have inherited Thy testimonies for ever, for they are the rejoicing of my heart. 112. I have inclined my heart to perform Thy statutes for ever for a recompense.*

Octave 14, v. 105-112: NUN. Tribe, father, founders of the family, etc.: There is relationship in the manifestations of spiritual life. Every virtue and vice have their ancestors and children, and the Prophet here speaks of them. God's revelation sanctifies faith (v. 105); from it comes the firm determination to serve God (v. 106), but in spite of her strong volition, the soul sees her weakness and humbles herself before God (v. 107). What is done with zeal is well done (v. 108). So disposed, the soul submits herself entirely to God's will (v. 109) and in spite of any obstacles, does not deviate from the law (v. 110). In the carrying out of God's commandments she finds great joy (v. 111) and soars on wings of hope of receiving the eternal reward from God (v. 112), according to our Saviour's Beatitudes.[2]

Since the only-begotten Word, coequal with the Father, is styled a light, and man when enlightened by the Word is also called a light, who is likewise styled a lamp, as John, as the apostles; and since no man of these is the Word, and that Word by whom they were enlightened is not a lamp, what is this word called a light and a lamp at the same time, except the word which was sent unto the prophets, or preached through the apostles? It was not Christ the Word, but the word of Christ, of which it is written: 'Faith cometh by hearing, and hearing by the word of God' (cf. Rom 10:17). For the Apostle Peter also, comparing the prophetical word to a lantern, says, 'whereunto ye do well that ye take heed, as unto a lantern, that shineth in a dark place' (2 Pet. 1:19). What, therefore, he calls 'Thy word' here, is the word which is contained in all the holy Scriptures.
Blessed Augustine of Hippo. OTP[5] (105), p. 577-578.

If someone possesses the *logos* of God and if he so uses the *logos* in speech and in every deed, even at the lifting of his foot to advance, such a man cannot stumble, for he possesses the 'lamp' and he sets [his course] thereby. If, on the contrary, he has received 'the lamp' and appears to give it faith but does not take it with him for every action and does not examine with the *logos* where to place his feet for every approach - the feet of his soul, if you will - that man commits a double fault, because he possesses the

logos and does not use it everywhere ...From one unique light are generated many lamps and each of those who possess by the grace of the *logos* of God this lighted lamp says: Do you seek a proof that Christ speaks in me? (cf. 2 Cor. 13:3). In all circumstances, therefore, one faith, which we have received, the *logos* of God, when we get ready to make a move, to speak, or to act, or in a thought, we will make use of the lamp to set out (cf. Lk. 8:16).
Attributed to Origen. LCP[4] pp. 359, 361.

SAMECH: *113. Transgressors have I hated, but Thy law have I loved. 114. My helper and my protector art Thou; on Thy words have I set my hope. 115. Depart from me, ye evil-doers, and I will search out the commandments of my God. 116. Uphold me according to Thy saying and quicken me, and turn me not away in shame from mine expectation. 117. Help me, and I shall be saved; and I will meditate on Thy statutes continually. 118. Thou hast set at nought all that depart from Thy statutes, for unrighteous is their inward thought. 119. I have reckoned as transgressors all the sinners of the earth, therefore have I loved Thy testimonies. 120. Nail down my flesh with the fear of Thee, for of Thy judgments am I afraid.*

Octave 15, v. 113-120: SAMECH. Support: Here is a discussion of dispositions and decisions of the will that serve as support of a God-pleasing life. The first such prop is the decision to love the law (v. 113), followed by the always ready assistance of the grace of God (v. 114). Firm determination and God's grace give boldness and make a strong man out of a weakling (v. 115). Trust, however, is not based on one's own strength, but on the assistance of God's grace (v. 116). These mainstays of a God-pleasing life are upheld by prayer (v. 117), the remembrance of God's non-sparing of sinners (v. 118), the cheerlessness of their lives (v. 119), and especially by the fear of God and the remembrance of God's judgments (v. 120).[2]

In the war we conduct against the devil and his demons, we have need of God's help. It is in a war of this kind that the Prophet has also gained help. God has protected him and this is why, prompted by grace, the psalmist pronounces these words. He adds that he has succeeded by the grace of God, 'on Thy words have I set my hope.' ...Those who hope do not rest in the state in which they commence to hope: since they progress towards God, they make their hope increase, and their hope grows in the same measure as the increase of their love; and it is above all when we are helped by God that we augment our hope relative to our desire for God.

I have found another explanation for the text: when I have faith in Your law and in Your prophets, I will hope in You, but when Your Christ has come among us, I have added to my hope in You the hope in Your Word, and I have redoubled my hope.

THE LAMENT OF EVE

Origen. LCP[4] p. 375.

After having said, 'depart from me, ye evil-doers,' logically he also invokes God's help for this, in order that, by his own strength the evil-doers should be repulsed in his soul, and that, in this respite, he may obtain life and salvation granted by God, without risk of a fall of his 'expectation.'
Eusebius of Caesarea. LCP[4] p. 377.

As another explains: he shows his imitation of God, if it is true that every man who departs from the judgments (of God) due to his vain thoughts is held for nought by God: to him also these people do not appear any better than common dregs or dross.
Apollonaris of Laodocia. LCP[4] p. 381.

He who is nailed is crucified. I therefore seek the cross and I wonder whether perhaps the cross is not the fear of God; and rightly the Saviour has said: 'He that taketh not his cross, and followeth after Me, is not worthy of Me' (Mt. 10:38). Many times, already, we have stated the difference between fear and love, and we have said that he who loves is more perfect than he who fears, and also that fear is necessary in the beginning until 'perfect love casteth out fear' (1 Jn. 4:18).
Origen. LCP[4] p. 381.

AIN: *121. I have wrought judgment and righteousness; O give me not up to them that wrong me. 122. Receive Thy servant unto good, let not the proud falsely accuse me. 123. Mine eyes have failed with waiting for Thy salvation, and for the word of Thy righteousness. 124. Deal with Thy servant according to Thy mercy, and teach me Thy statutes. 125. I am Thy servant; give me understanding, and I shall know Thy testimonies. 126. It is time for the Lord to act; for they have dispersed Thy law. 127. Therefore have I loved Thy commandments more than gold and topaz. 128. Therefore I directed myself according to all Thy commandments; every way that is unrighteous have I hated.*

Octave 16, v. 121-128: AIN. The Eye: The eye is the window of the soul. But there also is a spiritual eye which beholds the spiritual world: that is the mind or the spirit which perceives God, professes God's Providence, teaches obedience to God, longs for God and sees in God its ultimate happiness: this is the state of meditation. Here is the talk of the hopeful longing of the eyes of the heart and the mind towards God and of the devotion to the will of God in various circumstances which call out for such hope. The base of hope is devotion to God's will through fulfilment of His holy commandments ...The one who hopes has one eye directed towards God, awaiting His mercy, and the other upon the commandments, in order not to put an obstacle to this mercy.

If, after having sinned, I have not changed my life and 'wrought judgment,' and if, having rejected the wrong, I have not put the right in practice, You have reason -- since I have not converted myself -- to give me up to 'them that wrong me,' with a view to my chastisement. But since 'I have wrought judgment and righteousness,' I beg to be helped and not to be given up 'to them that wrong me' because of the sins I have committed. We should examine what is meant by "to be given up to." All faults which we commit, we commit by giving in to the devil who watches and lies in wait for the moment when [an opportunity arises] to introduce himself into our spirit, to throw his darts, and then come himself to occupy us and there exercise his action against us. When, after that, we sin ...it is incited by the devil, and we are violated by him.
Attributed to Origen LCP[4] p. 385.

Whoso therefore in the chaste fear of God has his flesh crucified, and corrupted by no carnal allurement, deals judgment and the work of righteousness, ought to pray that he may not be given up to his adversaries, that is, that he may not, through his dread of suffering evils, yield to his adversaries to do evil. For he receives power of endurance that guards him from being overcome with pain from Him from whom he receives the victory over lust, which prevents his being seduced by pleasure (cf. Ps. 61:5) ...
To prefigure His Cross, Moses by the merciful command of God, raised aloft on a pole the image of a serpent in the desert, so the likeness of sinful flesh which must be crucified in Christ might be prefigured (cf. Jn. 3:14). By gazing upon this healing cross, we cast out all the poison of the scandals of the proud: the cross, of which the Psalmist --intently looking upon it -- says: 'Mine eyes have failed with waiting for Thy salvation, and for the word of Thy righteousness' (v. 123). For God made Christ Himself 'to be sin for us, on account of the likeness of sinful flesh, that we may be made the righteousness of God in Him' (sic - cf. Rom 8:3). For His utterance of the righteousness of God he therefore says that his eyes have failed from gazing ardently and eagerly, while, remembering human infirmity, he longs for divine grace in Christ.
Blessed Augustine of Hippo OTP[5] (120, 122) p. 581, 582.

Why do these forces calumniate me? They are active in me and have persuaded me to sin, and it is they who accuse me in attributing to me all responsibility for my sins.
Origen LCP[4] p. 387.

Out of necessity he begs of God to be his protector, and so to speak his guarantor, so that He will become his guardian in guarding and protecting him ...to keep the calumniators who are watching for him, from gaining hold.

Eusebius of Caesaria LCP[4] p. 387.

Anew in this text, he calls the promise "teaching." I have continually awaited the salvation which comes from You; I am counting on the realization of Your promise. The verb 'have failed' has been employed to show the intensity of his desire.

Theodoret of Cyrus LCP[4] p. 389.

'Teach me Thy statutues.' This petition must never be intermitted. For it does not suffice to have received understanding, and to have learned the testimonies of God, unless it be always received, and for ever in a manner quaffed from the fountain of eternal light. For the testimonies of God are the better and the better known, the more understanding a man attains.

Grace has this object, that the commandments, which could not be fulfilled by fear, may be fulfilled by love ...Therefore, they are above gold and topaz stones. For this is read in another psalm also (cf. Ps. 18[19]:10) ...But those not understanding the hidden grace which was in the Old Testament, screened as it were by the veil (cf. Exo. 34:33-35; 2 Cor. 3:13-15) - this was signified when they were unable to gaze upon the face of Moses - endeavoured to obey the commandments of God for the sake of an earthly and carnal reward, but could not obey them. because they did not love them, but [loved] something else. So these were not the works of the willing, but rather the burdens of the unwilling. But when the commandments are loved for their own sake 'more than gold and topaz,' all earthly reward compared with the commandments themselves is vile, nor are any other goods of man comparable in any respect with those goods whereby man himself is made good.

Blessed Augustine of Hippo OTP[5] (124, 126): p. 581.

PE: *129. Wonderful are Thy testimonies; therefore hath my soul searched them out. 130. The unfolding of Thy words will give light and understanding unto babes. 131. I opened my mouth and drew in my breath, for I longed for Thy commandments. 132. Look upon me and have mercy on me, according to the judgment of them that love Thy name. 133. My steps do Thou direct according to Thy saying, and let no iniquity have dominion over me. 134. Deliver me from the false accusation of men, and I will keep Thy commandments. 135. Make Thy face to shine upon Thy servant, and teach me Thy statutes. 136. Mine eyes have poured forth streams of waters, because I kept not Thy law.*

EPILOGUE PART III: THE WAY, THE TRUTH AND THE LIFE

Octave 17, v. 129-136: PE. Mouth: God's mouth pronounces orders and commandments, the mouth of God-fearing people professes their absolute submission to God and they pray to Him to teach them and give them the strength to fulfill precisely all that is pronounced by His mouth, expressing contrition and repentance, if it ever will occur, to forsake it. God's words are wonderful and attract the attention of the soul (v. 129), the word of God makes wiser and enlightens (v. 130); the longing for God's commandments attracts His grace (v. 131). He who devotes himself to God finds himself under God's protection (v. 132), and the fear of the Lord protects him and guides him in his ways (v. 133). In the hour of trial it gives him the strength not to leave the path of virtue (v. 134), brings down upon him God's benevolence (v. 135), and bestows upon him the gift of tears for his sins (v. 136).[2]

Who counts, even by their kinds, the testimonies of God? Heaven and earth, His visible and invisible works, declare in some manner the testimony of His goodness and greatness; and the very ordinary and accustomed course of nature, whereby the seasons are rapidly revolved, in all things after their kinds, however temporal and perishable, however held cheap through our constant experience of them, give, if a pious thinker give heed to them, a testimony to the Creator. But which of these is not wonderful, if we measure each not by its habitual presence, but by reason? But if we venture to bring all nature within the comprehensive view of one act of contemplation, does not something take place in us that the Prophet describes, 'I considered Thy works, and was amazed' (cf. Hab. 3:2)? Yet the Psalmist was not terrified in his wonder at creation, but rather said that this was the reason that he ought to search it, because it was wonderful. For after saying, 'Thy testimonies are wonderful,' he adds, 'therefore hath my soul searched them out.'
Blessed Augustine of Hippo OTP[5] (128): p. 582.

Others, he says, admire gold and precious stones; I, as I know the divine orders are the only things admirable and beautiful, will keep to them and guard them above the importance of any treasure ...
The teachings need to be unveiled: that is why the Lord 'opened the understanding' of His disciples 'that they might understand the Scriptures' (Lk. 24:45). The understanding granted by the 'words' dispels the delusion which comes from pleasure or from vainglory.
Apollinaris of Laodicea LCP[4] pp. 399, 401.

What are the 'babes' but the humble and weak? Be not proud, therefore, presume not in your own strength, which is nothing, and you will understand why a good law was given by a good God, though it cannot give

life. For it was given for this end, that it might make you a little one instead of great, that it might show that you did not have strength to do the law out of your own power, and that, accordingly, wanting aid and destitute, you might fly towards grace, saying, 'Have mercy upon me, O Lord, for I am weak' (Ps. 6:2) ...Let all be little ones, and let all the world be guilty before You: because 'by the deeds of the law there shall no flesh be justified' in Your sight, 'for by the law is the knowledge of sin' etc. (cf. Rom 3:19-21). These are Your wonderful testimonies, which the soul of this little one has searched, and has therefore found, because he became humbled and a babe. For he does Your commandments as they ought to be done, that is by 'faith which worketh by love' (Gal. 5:6) unless love itself is shed abroad in his heart through the Holy Spirit (cf. Rom 5:5).
Blessed Augustine of Hippo OTP[5] (129): p. 582.

Another says: by 'babes' you should understand those who remain in ignorance and resemble nurslings. For it is they, he says, whom Your Word fills with intelligence when they are illumined with Your light.
Attibuted to Theodoret of Cyrus LCP[4] p. 401.

The first knowlege 'of Thy words,' that is to say Your teaching that is given to beginners, 'will give light and understanding unto babes.' Regarding 'Thy testimonies,' they are 'wonderful,' and they fill us with amazement. It is therefore in the proper position, having deployed the vessel of my soul and having 'opened' my mouth, I have received within myself the divine breath which comes from You, full of faith and Your promise, which says: 'Open thy mouth wide, and I will fill it' (Ps. 80:9).
Eusebius of Caesaria LCP[4] p. 401.

'The steps' of one who passes from vice and ignorance to virtue and to the knowledge of the truth are directed according to the sayings of God, for he who directs and guides such steps has right reasoning. So therefore, when it arrives, any iniquity in the man will not triumph. But it will triumph in one who repeats the iniquity, since it is said: 'Whosoever committeth sin is the servant of sin' (Jn. 8:34).
Attributed to Eusebius of Caesarea LCP[4] p. 405.

The Holy Scripture speaks of God in a material manner, because it conforms the words to human nature. Also it is necessary to wish for the manifestation of His divine 'face' - the deliverance from evil and bestowing of good.
Theodoret of Cyrus LCP[4] p. 407.

EPILOGUE PART III: THE WAY, THE TRUTH AND THE LIFE

TZADDI: *137. Righteous art Thou, O Lord, and upright are Thy judgments. 138. Thou hast ordained as Thy testimonies exceeding righteousness and truth. 139. My zeal for Thee hath made me to pine away, because mine enemies have forgotten Thy words. 140. Thine oracle is tried with fire to the uttermost, and Thy servant hath loved it. 141. I am young and accounted as nothing, yet Thy statutes have I not forgotten. 142. Thy righteousness is an everlasting righteousness, and Thy law is truth. 143. Tribulations and necessities have found me, Thy commandments are my meditation. 144. Thy testimonies are righteousness for ever; give me understanding and I shall live.*

Octave 18, v. 137-144: TZADDI. Flank or side: Here are indications of various sides, aspects or facets of the commandments; from each such side the relation to them is expressed by a specific disposition. Four of such dispositions are mentioned: Faith, the certainty that commandments are the truth and the immutable verity (v. 137, 138), zeal derived from such firm conviction and the desire to carry it out and the love of the commandments (v. 139, 140), humility with hope (v. 141, 142), endurance of anything that happens on account of faithfulness to commandments (v. 143, 144). Here is a complete program, and the bread of spiritual life is eaten in the midst of great spiritual effort.[2]

The righteousness of God and righteous judgment and truth, are to be feared by every sinner: for thereby all who are condemned are condemned of God; nor is there one who can righteously complain against the righteous God, of his own damnation. Therefore the tears of the penitent are needful, since if his impenitent heart were condemned, he would be most justly condemned. He indeed calls the testimonies of God righteousness: for he proves himself righteous by giving righteous commandments. And this is truth also, that God may become known by such testimonies.
Blessed Augustine of Hippo OTP[5] (136): p. 583.

Another says: He gives the reason he will weep over those who transgress the law; he threatens those who transgress with a chastisement before the divine tribunal and he renders testimony of it at this time by this text.
St. Athanasius of Alexandria LCP[4] p. 411.

What a great 'zeal' fills me when I see anyone forget 'Thy words'! And it was not a simple 'zeal,' but a zeal such that 'made me pine away' for You when I saw certain ones forget your words. And 'his disciples remembered' this zeal, for it is said in the Psalms: 'The zeal of Thine house hath eaten me up' (cf. Jn. 2:17; Ps. 68:12). If anyone forgets the words of God in the eyes of one who accomplishes the word of God with zeal, he is his enemy. 'As for them that hate Thee, O Lord, have I not hated them? And because of

Thine enemies have I not pined away? With perfect hatred have I hated them; they are reckoned enemies with me' (Ps. 138[137]:20, 21). Such was the sentiment of Elias when he said: 'I have been very jealous for the Lord Almighty' (3 Kings 19:10). Again, he is consumed by the zeal the Apostle tries to express to the Corinthians: 'For I am jealous over you with a godly jealousy' (2 Cor. 11:2).
Origen LCP[4] pp. 411, 413.

One can also say: ['Thine oracle'] is of fire, the celestial appearance from which Jesus came to send fire on the earth (cf. Lk. 12:49), the fire that devours as an herb all carnal disposition, of such a kind that it will consume the evil thoughts in us and render our soul pure, as gold is purified by fire.
Eusebius of Caesarea LCP[4] p. 413.

This is why the teaching 'tried with fire to the uttermost,' makes fervent of spirit (cf. Ps. 11:7) the one who loves it, because he is a 'servant of God.' This one, when Jesus explains the Scriptures, has a heart so much inflamed, that he can say, as Cleopas did: 'Did not our heart burn within us ...while He opened to us the Scriptures?'
St. Didymus the Blind LCP[4] pp. 413, 415.

Let us here recognize the two nations who were striving even in Rebecca's womb, when it was said to her, not from works, but of Him that calls: 'The elder shall serve the younger' (cf. Gen. 25:22, 23; Rom. 9:12). But the younger says here that he is of no reputation: for this reason he has become greater, since 'the last shall be first, and the first last' (Mt. 20:16).
It is no wonder that they have forgotten the words of God who have chosen to set up their own righteousness, ignorant of the righteousness of God (cf. Rom 10:3), but he, the younger, has not forgotten, for he has not wished to have a righteousness of his own, but that of God, of which he now also says, 'Thy righteousness is an everlasting righteousness, and Thy law is truth' (v. 142). For how is not the law truth, through which came the knowledge of sin, and that which gives testimony of the righteousness of God? For thus the Apostle says: 'The righteousness of God ...is manifested, being witnessed by the Law and the Prophets' (Rom 3:20, 21).
On account of this law the younger suffered persecution from the elder, so that the younger says what follows: 'Tribulations and necessities have found me, Thy commandments are my meditation.' Let them rage, let them persecute, as long as the commandments of God be not abandoned, and, after those commandments, let even those who rage be loved.
Blessed Augustine of Hippo OTP[5] (139 140, 141): pp. 583, 584.

My way, in effect, is narrow and strait 'which leadeth to life' (cf. Mt. 7:14). 'Many are the tribulations of the righteous, and the Lord shall deliver them out of them all' (Ps. 33[34]:19).
Attributed to Origen LCP[4] p. 417.

The testimonies which You have given me are not expedient for a little time: they are 'righteousness for ever,' since they justify those who approach them by the disposition of their hearts.
St. Didymus the Blind LCP[4] p. 419.

KOPH: *145. I have cried with my whole heart; hear me, O Lord, and I will seek after Thy statutes. 146. I have cried unto Thee; save me, and I will keep Thy testimonies. 147. I arose in the dead of night and I cried; on Thy words have I set my hope. 148. Mine eyes woke before the morning that I might meditate on Thy sayings. 149. Hear my voice, O Lord, according to Thy mercy; according to Thy judgment, quicken me. 150. They have drawn nigh that lawlessly persecute me, but from Thy law are they far removed. 151. Near art Thou, O Lord, and all Thy ways are truth. 152. From the beginning I have known from Thy testimonies that Thou hast founded them for ever.*

Octave 19, v. 145-152: KOPH. Ape: Imitation is not only necessary but indispensible in moral and religious life. Be merciful as your heavenly Father is merciful. The Prophet calls to imitate God as an example and at the same time as the giver of strength to imitate Him, and this is what all the invocations of this octave are about: 'I have cried with my whole heart,' hear me, save me, and I will seek Thy testimonies and keep them. He arises in the dead of the night to pray, and he gets up early to find the time to meditate; the enemies of spritual life persecute him, but he remains faithful to God, seeks Him and pledges always to be faithful to God's testimonies which have been established for ever.[2]

The cry is made a powerful noise by the importance of its message to God. The righteous does emit a strong sound towards God when he demands great and celestial things. It is as when the just Abel speaks from his death: 'The voice of thy brother's blood cries to Me out of the ground' (Gen. 4:10); which is said to show that the righteous has cried to God, putting out a powerful sound. And (God) says to Moses pursued by the Egyptians: 'Why criest thou to Me?' (Exo. 14:15). As for us, when we become saints, we have this cry within us: for the Spirit present in us cries 'Abba Father' (Rom. 8:15). And again, it is in this fashion that I hear the word: 'Jesus stood and cried, saying, If any man thirst, let him come unto Me and drink' (Jn. 7:37).

What is it then that cries to God? That which implores Him for great things and does not clamour for trivia.
  Origen LCP[4] p. 421.

This is the literal sense of the text [v 147]: I will not wait for the approach of day to pray, but "at the somber hour," in the night, I arose, before the signs of day, because, praying by night, I obtain a lift to my soul from the light of the truth, and, moreover, in my expectation, I have newly redoubled my hope in progressing in love, since love 'hopeth all things' (1 Cor. 13:7).
  Attributed to Origen LCP[4] p. 423.

You see, then, how near God is, but if we, even though He is close, do not make a move to approach Him, we do not enjoy His proximity. That is why the sinners are far from Him. 'For behold, they that remove themselves from Thee shall perish' (Ps. 72[73]:25) ...Moses approached God alone, the others did not come near (cf. Exo. 24:2). Those who approach God are linked to God according to the degree of their desire and of their perfection. It is of this that Paul speaks: 'But he that is joined unto the Lord is one spirit' (1 Cor. 6:17).
  Attributed to Origen LCP[4] p. 427.

Even in their troubles, it has been a usual confession of the saints, to ascribe truth to God, assuming they do not suffer them undeservedly. So did Queen Esther (cf. Esth. 14:6, 7), so did Holy Daniel (cf. Dan 9:4:16), so did the three men in the furnace (cf. Song of the Three Children 2-10), so do other associates in their sanctity confess. But it may be asked, in what sense it is said here: 'All Thy ways are truth,' since in another psalm it is read, 'All the ways of the Lord are mercy and truth' (cf. Ps. 24:10). But towards the saints, All the ways of the Lord are both mercy and truth: since He aids them even in judgment, and so mercy is not wanting, and in having mercy on them, He performs that which He has promised, so that truth is not wanting. But towards all, both those whom He frees, and those whom He condemns, all the ways of the Lord are mercy and truth, because where He does not show mercy, the truth of His vengeance is displayed. For He frees many who have not deserved, but He condemns none who has not deserved it.
  Blessed Augustine of Hippo OTP[5] (149): p. 585.

'The testimonies' were 'founded' by God in such a manner that none can loose or reverse them. Your Word, which is Your wisdom and Your Son, is their foundation. This is precisely why, in establishing their unshakable and indestructible character, He has said: 'Heaven and earth shall pass away, but My words shall not pass away' (Mt. 24:35; Mk. 13:31; Lk. 21:33).

EPILOGUE PART III: THE WAY, THE TRUTH AND THE LIFE

St. Didymus the Blind LCP[4] p. 429.

RESH: *153. Behold my humiliation and rescue me, for Thy law have I not forgotten. 154. Judge my cause and redeem me; for Thy word's sake quicken me. 155. Far from sinners is salvation, for they have not sought after Thy statutes. 156. Thy compassions are many, O Lord; according to Thy judgment quicken me. 157. Many are they that persecute me and afflict me; from Thy testimonies have I not declined. 158. I beheld men acting foolishly and I pined away, because they kept not Thy sayings. 159. Behold, how I have loved Thy commandments; O Lord, in Thy mercy, quicken me. 160. The beginning of Thy words is truth, and all the judgments of Thy righteousness endure for ever.*

Octave 20, v. 153-160: RESH. Head, meaning main, essential: In the moral life this word can be used to indicate the main dispositions of the heart by which such a life is upheld and activated. The Saviour pointed to such dispositions in His presentation of the Beatitudes: humility, contrition, meekness, love of truth, mercifulness, purity of heart, love of peace, patience, hope. And the Apostle Paul indicates similar dispositions when he enumerates the fruits of the Holy Spirit: love, joy, peace, long-suffering, gentleness, goodness, faith, meekness, temperance (Gal. 5:22, 23). And there are similar passages in other places of the Holy Scriptures, of which this octave is one. Shown here are humility, purity of the conscience, the seeking of God's statutes, hope of salvation, patience, zeal for the good morals of others, love of God and the conviction of the permanence of God's commandments.[2]

In many parts of the Scripture the word 'humiliation' is employed in speaking of trials, but it is also possible to understand by humiliation that which is opposed to arrogance: one who has confidence just because he has learned humility, and because the word has corrected him. He wants to invite God to regard the laudable humility realized in his soul. Everyone cannot say: 'for Thy law have I not forgotten,' but only he who has understood the law, who observes it always and invites God to regard the praiseworthy humility within his soul as well as the patience he demonstrates in trials: it is he who can effectively say 'Thy law have I not forgotten' ...

Why? Because of themselves. Indeed it is written: 'Behold, they that remove themselves from Thee shall perish' (Ps. 72[73]:25), for it is not salvation that escapes us, but we who flee salvation. 'The Son of man' who is salvation 'is come to seek and to save that which was lost' (Lk. 19:10). 'Far from sinners is salvation': what is the reason for it? It is 'for they have not sought after Thy statutes.' If, therefore, someone does not seek after the statutes of God, far from him is salvation, which comes from God ...

THE LAMENT OF EVE

There is a useful expression stated by the Apostle, and proclaimed not once but many times in the Scripture: 'all that will live godly in Christ Jesus shall suffer persecution' (2 Tim. 3:12) ...The just, consequently, does not cease to be persecuted; he does not cease to testify in front of the invisible powers, in the secret of his heart. It is of these testimonies the Apostle says: 'For our rejoicing is this, the testimony of our conscience' (2 Cor. 1:12).
Origen LCP[4] pp. 431, 433, 435, 437.

Where there is a beginning, I look for what comes after the beginning, until I arrive at the end. And in the same way, in relation to the word 'the fear of the Lord is the beginning of wisdom' (Ps. 110:9), since the fear of the Lord is the beginning of wisdom, I look for what comes after the beginning and that should be superior to fear and better. I find that it is love, in the same fashion as here. If it is true that the beginning of the words of God is 'truth,' what could best come after this commencement? And the end of the beginning that is 'truth,' what could that be? When we are neophytes, we receive the truth, but without the knowledge that establishes the truth with certainty and without the reasoning that demonstrates this truth. That is why the beginning of the words which man receives for his salvation is not 'wisdom,' the beginning is not reason, but 'truth.'
It is thus, for example, that the catechumen learns as an elementary teaching: 'one God and Father of all, who is above all, and through all, and in you all' (Eph. 4:6). He is taught that Christ was sent 'in the end of the world ...to put away sin by the sacrifice of Himself' (cf. Heb. 9:26); He was born miraculously from a virgin; that He suffered on the cross for all men, that He was resurrected from the dead on the third day.
Attributed to Origen LCP[4] pp. 439, 441.

SCHIN: *161. Princes have persecuted me without a cause, and because of Thy words my heart hath been afraid. 162. I will rejoice in Thy sayings as one that findeth great spoil. 163. Unrighteousness have I hated and abhorred, but Thy law have I loved. 164. Seven times a day have I praised Thee for the judgments of Thy righteousness. 165. Much peace have they that love Thy law, and for them there is no stumbling-block. 166. I awaited Thy salvation, O Lord, and Thy commandments have I loved. 167. My soul hath kept Thy testimonies and hath loved them exceedingly. 168. I have kept Thy commandments and Thy testimonies, for all my ways are before Thee, O Lord.*

Octave 21, v. 161-168: SCHIN. Tooth: In the animal kingdom teeth are the instruments of protection and feeding, and in addition to that, they help human beings to speak. What means of protection are given a person who wants to live by the commandments of God? Fear of transgressing the law (v. 161), hope for the blessings resulting from its fulfilling (v. 162), love of the law (v. 163). These fill the soul and mind with praise to God for the blessings from the judgments of God's truth (v. 164), and those blessings which are imparted as the result of fulfilling God's commandments: peace of mind (v. 165), hope of salvation (v. 166), the very love of the commandments (v. 167), and the final crowning of everything: to walk before God (v. 168).[2]

Let us behold the martyr: he does not regard the diverse instruments of torture and he is not alarmed, but recollects the judgment of God and fears it, and he is entirely occupied in presenting to himself this judgment and the chastisements reserved above for those who deny God. He also says 'princes have persecuted me without a cause,' not because I am a thief or a murderer, or because I have committed some reprehensible act, but because I honour You, God, You, the creator of the universe, because I have believed in the name of Your Only-Begotten Son, for this cause I am persecuted, and in this persecution I have fear, not because of them nor the menaces they proffer, but because of the awe that I feel for Your words.
Origen LCP[4] p. 447.

How then have the Christians offended against them? What due have they not rendered? In what have not Christians obeyed the monarchs of earth? The kings of the earth therefore have persecuted the Christians without a cause. They too had their threatening words: I banish, I proscribe, I slay, I torture with claws, I burn with fires, I expose to beasts, I tear the limbs piecemeal. But heed what he has subjoined: 'and because of Thy words my heart hath been afraid.' My heart has stood in awe of these words, 'Fear not them that kill the body' (cf. Mt. 10:28). I have scorned man who persecutes me, and have overcome the devil that would seduce me ...
The words of God are no other than the law of God. Far be it therefore from love to perish through fear, where fear is chaste. Thus fathers are both feared and loved by affectionate sons; thus does a chaste wife both fear her husband, lest she be forsaken by him, and love him, so she may enjoy his love. If then the human father and the human husband desire both to be feared and loved, much more does our Father who is in heaven, and that Bridegroom, 'beautiful beyond the sons of men' (cf. Ps. 44:2), not in the flesh, but in goodness. For by whom is the law of God loved, save by those by whom God is loved? ...Let the Father's judgments therefore be praised even in the scourge, if His promises be loved in the reward.
Blessed Augustine of Hippo OTP[5] (159, 161), pp. 586, 587.

Since he has mentioned enemies who persecute him, in the proper place he has also introduced the mention of spoils. He wants to say: if I

were to kill them all and if I collected all the spoils taken on them, I would not rejoice as much as I am gladdened in Your laws.
Theodoret of Cyrus LCP[4] p. 449.

The words 'seven times a day,' signify "evermore." For this number is wont to be a symbol of universality, because after six days of the divine work of creation, a seventh of rest was added (cf. Gen. 2:2), and all times roll on through a revolving cycle of seven days. For no other reason it was said, 'a righteous man will fall seven times, and rise again' (Prov. 24:16), that is, the just man does not perish though brought low in every way, yet not induced to transgress, otherwise he will not be just. For the words, 'falleth seven times,' are employed to express every kind of tribulation, whereby man is cast down in the sight of men, and the words 'riseth up again,' signify that he profits from all these tribulations.
Blessed Augustine of Hippo OTP[5] (162), p. 587.

One can understand again, in observing this: rising from his couch before the sun, in imitation of him who said: 'With my soul have I desired Thee in the night, my God' (cf. Isa. 26:9) and 'O God, my God, unto Thee I rise at dawn' (Ps. 62[63]:1), he addresses to God his first hymn. Afterwards, when day has come, at the first hour, as a morning sacrifice, he offers to God the second hymn; likewise at the third hour the third hymn, at the sixth hour, anew, the fourth hymn; at the ninth hour the fifth; at the twelfth, the sixth; and then at evening, after having tended to his body, at the moment he gains his couch, he acquits himself of a seventh hymn and completes this verse: 'seven times a day have I praised Thee.'
Eusebius of Caesarea LCP[4] pp. 451, 453.

If therefore those who loved God's commandments waited for His saving health, how much more necessary was Jesus, that is, the saving Health of God, for the salvation of those who did not love His command-ments? This prophecy may also suit the saints of the period since the revelation of grace, and the preaching of the Gospel, for those who love God's commandments look for Christ, so 'when Christ, our life, shall ap-pear, we' may then 'appear with Him in glory' (Col. 3:4).
Blessed Augustine of Hippo OTP[5] (164), p. 587.

TAU: *169. Let my supplication draw nigh before Thee, O Lord; according to Thine oracle give me understanding. 170. Let my petition come before Thee, O Lord; according to Thine oracle deliver me. 171. My lips shall pour forth a hymn when Thou hast taught me Thy statutes. 172. My tongue shall speak of Thy sayings, for all Thy commandments are righteousness. 173. Let Thy hand be for saving me, for I have chosen Thy commandments. 174. I*

have longed for Thy salvation, O Lord, and Thy law is my meditation. 175.
My soul shall live and shall praise Thee, and Thy judgments will help me.
176. I have gone astray like a sheep that is lost; O seek Thy servant, for I have
not forgotten Thy commandments.

Octave 22, v. 169-176: TAU. Sign: Here indicated are signs by which
one can determine if one is on the right track and whether one is walking
along it in the right way. This is the last and conclusive octave. It describes
the height of human perfection, the fruits borne by a soul devoted to God.
It has learned to pray, to seek understanding and help from God (v. 169,
170), on account of which ardent prayer and praise to God are bursting
from the soul (v. 171), and the tongue wants to declare God's ways to other
people (v. 172). The assurance of God's protection gives daring and in-
creases zeal for salvation (v. 173, 174), as it quickens the soul and fills it
with assuredness that God will help unto the end (v. 175), yet, at the last
moment the Prophet humbles himself before God and appeals to His mercy
(v. 176). And that is the very best sign of his salvation.[2]

Let us now hear the words of one praying, since we know who is praying, and we recognize ourselves, if we are not reprobate, among the members of this one praying ...He claims a promise. For he says, 'according to
Thine oracle,' which is to say, according to Thy promise. For the Lord
promised this when He said, 'I will instruct thee' (Ps. 31:8).
Blessed Augustine of Hippo OTP[5] (166), p. 588.

All along in the foregoing letters he journeyed towards God and has
not yet come near Him. When he has come to the last letter of the present
text and the last letter of the Hebrew alphabet, he begs in a prayer that his
supplication 'draw nigh' before God and may reach Him. In order to 'draw
nigh' to God, you must know that we have discerned the following differences: the perfect approach God in person; those who are less than perfect
but near perfect, do not come near God in person, but it is their prayer that
approaches God. That is why these words are found in the case of Moses:
'And Moses alone shall come near the Lord; but they shall not come nigh'
(Exo. 24:2), whereas, in the case of the Prophet, his prayer says 'Let my
petition come before Thee, O Lord.'
The nature of the difference is worth the effort now to examine. God is
not in a place, for He certainly is not a body, but a power ineffable, inexpressible and invisible; so if God is not in a place and if it is in no way possible to 'draw nigh' to God, it is clear that it is by means of the invisible element within ourselves that we approach Him. But what is that invisible element within but 'the hidden man of the heart' (cf. 1 Pet. 3:4) that the Scripture has called 'the inner man' (cf. Eph. 3:16, Rom. 7:22). It is to him, in

fact, that he returns to approach God. One can 'draw nigh' through Jesus Christ as the intermediary, and particularly if one understands that Christ is righteousness, that He is truth, wisdom, resurrection, and the true light, for without that one cannot approach God any more than without the peace that keeps the heart and mind through Christ Jesus (cf. Phil. 4:7) ...Moses, then, did not 'draw nigh' to God spatially, but having an interior disposition such that he was close to God.

Attributed to Origen LCP[4] pp. 457, 459.

We know how God teaches those who are docile towards God. For every one who has heard from the Father and has learned, comes unto Him 'who justifieth the ungodly' (Rom. 4:5), so that he may keep the righteousness of God not only by retaining them in his memory, but also by doing them. So he who glories, does not glory himself, but in the Lord (cf. 1 Cor. 1:31), and bursts forth praise ...

When he says that he will declare these things, he becomes a minister of the word. For though God teaches within, nevertheless 'faith cometh from hearing: and how do they hear without a preacher?' (Rom. 10:17, 14). For, because 'God giveth the increase' (1 Cor. 3:7) is no reason why we need not plant and water ...

Thus God saved the martyrs, when he did not permit them to be slain in their souls, for 'vain is the salvation of man' (Ps. 59[60]:12) in the flesh. The words 'Let Thy hand be for saving me' may also be taken to mean Christ the Hand of God ...

'I have longed for Thy salvation' ...let Christ the salvation of God occur to us. The righteous men of old confess that they longed for Him, the Church longed for His destined coming from His mother's womb, the Church longs for His coming at His Father's right hand. Subjoined to this sentence are the words, 'And Thy law is my meditation,' for the Law gives testimony unto Christ.

Blessed Augustine of Hippo OTP[5] (169, 170), p. 588.

Your divers 'sayings,' which prescribe the particular virtues, altogether constitute a unique reality, which comprises virtue in general, from the point that the particular virtues link themselves to one another in such a way that when one possesses one perfectly, one possesses them all.

St. Didymus the Blind LCP[4] p. 465.

I wonder what is the 'hand' of God about which he addresses this prayer. With His powerful hand, God made Israel leave Egypt (cf. Exo. 13:9). What is that hand? Christ Jesus, for He is the hand and the law of God.

Origen LCP[4] p. 467.

You will only bring to life that soul which now lives by You and not by the world.

You will only preserve that body, which has begun to be filled with the Holy Spirit during this time (cf. Phil. 3:10-11, 20-21).

That which is of the Living God in the graves, will be resurrected into life.

No one can resurrect the dead except the Lord, and no one can rise from the dead except the Lord.

For He is in His holy people. Truly, He is in His living people, both in the grave and out of the grave.

Bishop Nikolai Velimirovich. *Prayers by the Lake* (XVII). Treasury of Serbian Orthodox Spirituality, Vol. V, translated by Rt. Rev. Todor Mika and V. Rev. Dr. Stevan Scott, p. 183.

(My soul shall live) for remembering Your judgments and keeping them, I avoid the death that follows on sin; I never sin again, to the contrary, I accomplish those deeds of which the consequence will be: 'my soul shall live and shall praise Thee,' in giving thanks for eternal life which You have given it.

St. Didymus the Blind LCP[4] p. 471.

I know that Your judgments, frightening as they are for others, will come to my aid, for He renders to each according to his works (cf. Rom. 2:16, Mt. 16:27, Ps. 61:11, Prov. 24:12).

Eusebius of Caesarea LCP[4] p. 471.

At last he opens himself completely, and shows what person was speaking throughout the whole psalm ...Let the lost sheep be sought, let the lost sheep be quickened ...As for that company, among whom the Psalmist says, 'I have not forgotten Thy commandments,' it has been found, but through those who choose the commandments of God, gather them together, love them, it is still sought, and by means of the blood of its shepherd shed and sprinkled abroad, it is found in all nations.

Blessed Augustine of Hippo OTP[5] (172), pp. 588, 589.

'Like a sheep that is lost' one among the hundred which the Saviour went to seek, leaving the ninety nine others on the mountains (cf. Mt. 18:12, Lk. 15:4), the Psalmist has strayed, from the fact of the transgression of Adam, for the lost sheep, one of a hundred -- that is mankind. As for the rational beings, who have not fallen, those who are also part of creation, they rest on the mountains, thanks to the loftiness of their virtues, and to the doctrines of truth, in so far as only man has a part in wandering. Since, therefore, I have erred in the same way as the lost sheep, or rather then

149

THE LAMENT OF EVE

being a party to this lost sheep, seek me, 'O seek Thy servant,' for You are 'come to seek and to save that which was lost' (Lk. 19:10, Mt. 18:11). Seek me to find me, for I am disposed towards it since I have ardently desired Thy commandments.

St. Didymus the Blind LCP[4] pp. 471, 473.

Having spoken of those works which he has accomplished rightly, he then speaks of himself as a lost sheep, thereby practicing humility.

St. Athanasius of Alexandria LCP[4] p. 473.

The Prophet has uttered this word, but it is mankind in its entirety that has received salvation. For the Good Shepherd (cf. Jn. 10:11) has run to the meeting with the errant sheep, He has traversed the mountains and valleys (it is indeed in these regions that it errs, in service to demons). He has found it, and carrying it on His shoulders, he has brought it back and has in it more joy than in the ninety nine others that have not erred (cf. Lk. 15:4-6).

Theodoret of Cyrus LCP[4] p. 473.

Since 'Christ is the end of the law for righteousness' (Rom. 10:4), the Prophet has done well to declare the present verse as a seal for this psalm, and he pronounces it in the name of humanity as a whole. 'All we as sheep have gone astray; everyone has gone astray in his own way' (Isa. 53:6), as has been lucidly expressed by Isaiah. Not only have we erred, but we are even lost -- the enemy has ruined us, he has directed our wandering; to deceit he has added delusion; he has added evil to evil; he has deepened the abyss of our need, but the real shepherd has not rejected us even in this situation, 'for the Son of man is come to seek and to save that which is lost' (Lk. 19:10), as our Lord Himself said.

St. Hesychius of Jerusalem LCP[4] p. 473.

+

"Oh, that you would bear with me in a little folly - and indeed you do bear with me. For I am jealous for you with godly jealousy. For I have betrothed you to one husband, that I may present you as a chaste virgin to Christ. But I fear, lest somehow, as the serpent deceived Eve by his craftiness, so your minds may be corrupted from the simplicity that is in Christ."

St. Paul: Second Letter to the Corinthians 11:1-3.

INDEX OF CHURCH FATHERS/COMMENTATORS

Shown below is a listing of patristic commentators used in this book, together with the approximate dates of their death, as indicated by " + ". Under the page numbers, "G" indicates their commentary was on the Book of Genesis, and "P" indicates commentary on Psalm 118.

COMMENTATORS   PAGES

St, Ambrose of Milan (+ 397)   G 34

Apollinaris of Laodicea* (+ 390)   P 109, 115, 117, 126, 128, 134, 137

St. Athanasius of Alexandria (+ 373) G 10, 18, 31; P 111, 120, 123, 125, 129, 139, 150

Blessed Augustine of Hippo** (+ 430)   G 11, P 109, 110, 112, 113, 114, 115, 117, 118, 120, 123, 124, 127, 128, 129, 130, 132, 135, 136, 137, 138, 139, 140, 142, 145, 146, 147, 148, 149

St. Basil the Great (+ 379)   G 1-6, 11

St. Diadochos of Photiki (+ 485) G 7

St. Didymus the Blind* (+ 398)   G 7-9, 25-26, 48; P 109, 111, 117, 122, 123, 124, 130, 131, 140, 141, 143, 148, 149, 150

Eusebius of Caesarea (+ 340)   P 111, 115, 119, 127, 134, 136, 138, 140, 146, 149

St. Gregory of Nazianzus (+ 389) G 17-18, 24-25

St. Gregory of Nyssa (+ 396)   G 9-10, 49

St. Hesychius of Jerusalem (+ ca.450) P 150

St. Hilary of Poitiers (+ 368)   P 108, 110, 112, 115, 116, 119, 121, 122

St. Irenaeus of Lyons (+202)   G 31-33

St. John Cassian (+ 435)   P 113

St. John Chrysostom (+ 407)   G 6-7, 16-17, 18, 21-24, 28-30, 36-39, 44-48; P 125

St. John Climacus (+ ca.649)   P 112

St. John of Damascus (+ 749)   G 13-15

St. Maximus the Confessor (+ 662) G 11-12

Bishop Nikolai Velimirovich (+ 1956) G 19, 26, 31, 42-43, 49; P 149

Origen* (+ ca.234)   P 111, 114, 119, 120, 129, 131, 133, 134, 135, 140, 141, 142, 144, 145, 148

St. Symeon the New Theologian (+ 1022)   G 6, 15-16, 26-28

Theodoret of Cyrus* (+ 466)   P 122, 128, 131, 136, 138, 146, 150

St. Theophan the Recluse (+ 1894) P 108, 110, 112, 114, 116, 118, 120, 121, 123, 126, 127, 129, 130, 132, 133, 134, 137, 139, 141, 143, 144, 147

*Note: The commentators listed above, with an asterisk had other writings or associations which included material condemned as heretical by the Church. Every effort has been made to avoid this material or writings having ideas associated therewith. The reader is cautioned accordingly.
** Doctrinal differences exist between Orthodox and Roman Catholic Christians regarding some of the writings of Blessed Augustine on subjects such as grace, free will, original sin, and the procession of the Holy Spirit. For an explanation of these differences, see Vladimir Lossky THE MYSTICAL THEOLOGY OF THE EASTERN CHURCH, and Protopresbyter Michael Pomazansky ORTHODOX DOGMATIC THEOLOGY.

BIBLIOGRAPHY

Ancient Christian Writers, (ACW) Edited by Johannes Quasten, S.T.D. et al. and various translators, 53 Volumes, © Paulist Prest, Mahway, N.J. 07430. Used by permission of Paulist Press.
The Ante-Nicene Fathers (ANF), 10 Volumes, Wm. B. Eerdmans Publishing Company, Grand Rapids 1989.
The Bible and the Holy Fathers for Orthodox, compiled and edited by Johanna Manley, Monastery Books 1990 - see next page.
La Chaîne Palestinienne sur le Psaume 118, 2 Volumes, transl. into French by Marguerite Harl, Sources Chrétiennes (SC) #189, 190, © Les Éditions du Cerf, Paris 1972.
The Classics of Western Spirituality (CWS), 60 + Volumes, various translations. © Paulist Press, Mahway, NJ 07430. Used by permission.
The Fathers of the Church (CUA), 83 + Vols., © Catholic University of America Press, Washington, D.C. 1953. Used by permission.
Grace for Grace: The Psalter and the Holy Fathers, compiled and edited by Johanna Manley, Monastery Books - see next page.
The Nicene and Post-Nicene Fathers (NPNF), First Series (FS) and Second Series (SS), 28 Volumes, Wm. B. Eerdmans Publishing Company, Grand Rapids, MI.
Sur la Genèse, Didyme l'Aveugle, Tomes I, II, transl. into French by Pierre Nautin. Sources Chrétiennes #233, 244, © Les Éditions du Cerf, Paris, 1976, 1978.
Sur l'Origine de l'Homme, Basile de Césarée, transl. into French by Alexis Smets, S.J. and Michel Van Esbroeck, S.J. Sources Chrétiennes #160. © Les Éditions du Cerf, Paris 1970.
The Philokalia, Vols. 1, 2, 3, compiled by St. Nicodemos of the Holy Mountain and St. Makarios of Corinth, Faber and Faber, London 1979, 1980.
The Prologue from Ochrid, Vols. 1, 2, 3, 4, transl. by Mother Maria. © Lazarica Press, Birmingham, England and Mother Maria 1985.
The Psalter According to the Seventy, translated from the Septuagint Version of the Old Testament, © 1974 by Holy Transfiguration Monastery, Brookline, MA. Used by permission.
The Septuagint with Apocrypha Greek and English, transl. by Sir Lancelot C. L. Brenton, Hendrickson Publishers, Peabody, MA 1990.
The Sin of Adam, Seven Homilies by St. Symeon the New Theologian, pub. and © by Saint Herman of Alaska Brotherhood, Platina, CA 1979.
Sources Chrétiennes Series, 368 + Volumes (French), © Les Éditions du Cerf, 29, Bd. de Latour-Maubourg, Paris-7e, France.
A Treasury of Serbian Orthodox Spirituality (TSOS), 5 Volumes, translated by Rt. Rev. Todor Mika and Very Rev. Dr. Stevan Scott, Serbian Orthodox New Gracanica Metropolitanate, Grayslake, IL 1988-1990.
The Collected Works of Bishop Nikolai (Velimirović), 12 Volumes (Serbian), Izdanje Srpske Pravoslavne Eparhije Zapadioevropske, Chimelstir, 1986.

Illustration:
The traditional Orthodox "Holy Saturday" icon on the cover is from St. Vladimir's Seminary, Crestwood, NY.

OTHER BOOKS FROM MONASTERY BOOKS:

THE BIBLE AND THE HOLY FATHERS FOR ORTHODOX
COMPILED AND EDITED BY JOHANNA MANLEY
Foreword by Bishop Kallistos of Diokleia; Preface by Archpriest John Breck, Professor, St. Vladimir's Orthodox Theological Seminary.
In compiling this work, the Orthodox liturgical calendar was used as a basis for the best means both to encourage daily devotions and to convey the flow - including feasts and fasts - of the Orthodox life style.
This work contains the New Testament scriptural readings (NKJV) prescribed by the Church for ever day of the year for the movable calendar, starting with Easter, the Feast of Feasts. There are also many sections of the Old Testament to support the lectionary for major feast days, Great Lent, and Holy Week. Supplementing each Epistle and Gospel text are commentaries from one or more of 79 Holy Fathers, most from the first fourteen centuries A.D. In addition, writings from many contemporary Orthodox (Russian, Serbian, Greek) theologians, scholars, and clergy are included.
Three Appendices are provided: Matins readings about the Resurrection; lections for Major Fixed Feasts; and General readings for saints, martyrs, Commemoration of the Dead - all with commentary or references. Copious iconic illustrations.
The Indices comprise 62 pages: (1) Holy Fathers and Contemporary Authors, and their topics; (2) Concordance of Scripture passage and time of reading according to the lectionary; (3) Subjects Index; (4) Bible Study; Harmony of the Gospels and Guidelines. Detailed source indications are given, tied to the Bibliography, for further pursuit of study of the commentary material.

GRACE FOR GRACE; THE PSALTER AND THE HOLY FATHERS
COMPILED AND EDITED BY JOHANNA MANLEY
Foreword by Archimandrite Todor Mika, Serbian Orthodox Monastery of the Holy Cross, Castro Valley, CA.

This very Christ-centered book provides a new, yet ancient view of the Psalter. It offers an anthology of commentary by the Church Fathers--through direct commentary and proof texts--and of meditations relating to the Psalms and scriptural Odes. Numerous illustrations are from 11th and 12th-century Greek Psalters and from a 15th-century Serbian Psalter. Psalms were often used within the words of Christ and His apostles. This same intimate association carried through to the liturgical services. Extracts from Orthodox Christian festal and lenten services have also been included as heuristic aids, as well as some Old Testament passages (LXX) from the Book of Kings. In addition to the early patristic commentary and meditations, the contemporary writings of Bishop Nikolai Velimirovich have been interwoven into each chapter.
Included also within this volume are the following: THE PSALTER ACCORDING TO THE SEVENTY - a Septuagint version translated by Holy Transfiguration Monastery, Brookline, MA. Two Appendices outling differences between the Septuagint and Hebrew versions; the Psalms and Odes in common liturgical use; and a Glossary. Eight Indices: Psalmic and Commentary Themes; Sources--patristic and service books; a Liturgical Concordance detailing the use of Psalms in Orthodox Christian, Roman Catholic, and Episcopalian festal and lenten services (25 Pages); Subjects; Scriptural Texts Cited, and Bibliography.

Write to **MONASTERY BOOKS**, P.O. Box 2579, 287 Bay Road, Menlo Park, CA for further information.

153